Web 3.0 and Decentralized Technologies

Shaping the Future of the Internet

Author: Martin Hander

Publication Date: 20231030

Pictures: pixabay.com

Copyright 2023 Martin Hander

Preface

Welcome to the world of Web 3.0 and Decentralized Technologies. As you embark on this journey through the digital frontier, you are about to delve into the very heart of a technological revolution that promises to reshape the way we interact with the online world.

The internet, since its inception, has undergone dramatic transformations. From the early days of static web pages to the dynamic, user-driven content of Web 2.0, we have witnessed the power of human connection and the exchange of information on a global scale. Now, we stand at the cusp of a new era, an era that is decentralized, secure, and poised to revolutionize not only the digital realm but the very fabric of our society.

The Promise of Web 3.0

In "Web 3.0 and Decentralized Technologies," we explore the foundations, principles, and innovations that are driving the transition to a decentralized web. The internet as we know it is a centralized ecosystem, where power, data, and control are concentrated in the hands of a few. Web 3.0 challenges this centralization, bringing forth technologies like blockchain, smart contracts, and decentralized applications (DApps) to empower individuals and communities.

Our journey begins with an introduction to Web 3.0, outlining its potential and the key concepts that underpin it. We delve into the intricacies of blockchain technology, which serves as the backbone of decentralized systems. From understanding cryptographic principles to exploring real-world use cases, you'll gain a deep appreciation of this transformative technology.

Decentralized Applications: The New Frontier

DApps, short for decentralized applications, are at the forefront of the Web 3.0 revolution. These applications run on decentralized networks, granting users more control over their data and digital experiences. We explore the birth of DApps, how they function, and the myriad ways they can disrupt traditional industries.

The transition to a decentralized internet doesn't stop at financial services or applications. In this book, you'll also discover how Web 3.0 is revolutionizing digital identity, supply chain management, content publishing, and more. The potential for innovation and disruption in these areas is immense, and you'll be equipped with the knowledge to navigate this evolving landscape.

The Road Ahead

While the promise of Web 3.0 and decentralized technologies is exhilarating, it's not without its challenges. Scalability issues, regulatory hurdles, and the need for widespread user adoption are among the obstacles we'll explore. Additionally, we'll delve into the governance of decentralized systems and the importance of interoperability and standards to ensure a seamless transition to the decentralized internet.

As you journey through these pages, you'll gain insights into the future of Web 3.0. Anticipated technological advances, transformations in industry and business, and the profound societal impact of this transition are all part of the discussion. More than just a technological shift, Web 3.0 holds the potential to redefine the way we live, work, and interact in the digital world.

Join the Revolution

This book is your passport to the future, a future where the internet belongs to the people, where security and privacy are paramount, and where innovation knows no bounds. As you read, learn, and absorb the content within these pages, we invite you to become an active participant in the journey toward Web 3.0.

The author's mission is to guide you through the complexities of this evolving landscape, break down the barriers to understanding, and empower you to harness the potential of decentralized technologies. Your role in this revolution is not passive; it's participatory. The future of the internet is being written, and you are invited to be one of its authors.

So, let's embark on this transformative journey together, as we explore the concepts, technologies, and implications of Web 3.0 and decentralized technologies. The future of the internet is in your hands, and we're excited to see where it takes us.

About the Author

Martin Hander

Martin Hander is a seasoned software developer and visionary tech enthusiast with over two decades of experience. With a strong foundation in computer science, their journey in the world of technology has been marked by innovation, problem-solving, and a passion for exploring the frontiers of digital transformation.

After obtaining a degree in computer science from a prestigious institution, Martin Hander embarked on a professional journey that took them through diverse industries and sectors. Their adaptability and skillset allowed them to thrive in a variety of companies, each with its unique challenges and opportunities. Over the years, they've contributed to the success of projects spanning [List of Industries/Fields], leaving their mark on the ever-evolving tech landscape.

Beyond the confines of code and development, Martin Hander finds solace and inspiration in the simplicity of life's pleasures. In their free time, you can often find them outdoors, exploring the world with their loyal canine companion. The bond with their dog reflects a deeper connection to the values of loyalty and companionship, which are woven into the fabric of their personal and professional life.

Family is at the heart of Martin Hander's world. They cherish moments spent with loved ones, finding balance and fulfillment in the shared joys of life. This dedication to family extends to the broader tech community, where Martin Hander is committed to helping others navigate the complexities of Web 3.0 and decentralized technologies.

With this book, Martin Hander aims to distill their extensive knowledge and real-world experiences into an accessible guide for those seeking to understand and embrace the future of the internet. Their unique perspective as a software developer, combined with a deep appreciation for life's simple pleasures, makes this book a bridge to the exciting world of Web 3.0 and decentralized technologies.

Table of Contents

Preface 2
   The Promise of Web 3.0 2
   Decentralized Applications: The New Frontier 3
   The Road Ahead 4
   Join the Revolution 5
About the Author 6
Chapter 1: Introduction to Web 3.0 12
   1.1 The Evolution of the Web 12
   1.2 The Centralized Web's Limitations 14
   1.3 The Promise of Web 3.0 17
   1.4 Key Concepts in Web 3.0 21
   1.5 Web 3.0 Use Cases 25
Chapter 2: Blockchain Technology 29
   2.1 The Fundamentals of Blockchain 29
   2.2 Cryptography and Security 32
   2.3 Blockchain Consensus Mechanisms 35
   2.4 Smart Contracts: The Digital Backbone of Web 3.0 39
   2.5 Use Cases for Blockchain 42
Chapter 3: Decentralized Applications (DApps) 46
   3.1 The Birth of DApps 47
   3.2 How DApps Work: The Mechanics of Decentralized Applications 50
   3.3 Types of DApps: Pioneering Decentralized Solutions .. 54
   3.4 Benefits and Challenges of DApps 58
   3.5 Real-World DApp Examples 62
Chapter 4: The Decentralized Internet - Navigating the Web 3.0 Landscape 65
   4.1 Web 3.0 and Internet Decentralization: A Paradigm Shift 67
   4.2 Decentralized File Storage: Empowering Data Ownership 70

4.3 Decentralized Domain Name Systems: Reimagining Internet Identity 74
4.4 Building a Decentralized Internet: Navigating Web 3.0's Vision 77
4.5 Future Possibilities: Pioneering the Uncharted Territories of Web 3.0 81
Chapter 5: Blockchain-Based Identity and Privacy 84
5.1 The Challenge of Digital Identity 84
5.2 Self-Sovereign Identity: Taking Control of Your Digital Persona 87
5.3 Privacy and Data Ownership: Web 3.0's Cornerstones . 90
5.4 Decentralized Identity Platforms: The Key to Secure, User-Centric Identity 93
5.5 Identity and Web 3.0: A Paradigm Shift in Blockchain-Based Identity and Privacy 96
Chapter 6: Web 3.0 and Finance 99
6.1 Decentralized Finance (DeFi): Transforming the Financial World in Web 3.0 100
6.2 Cryptocurrencies and Digital Assets: The New Currency of Web 3.0 Finance 102
6.3 Automated Finance (Afi): The Future of Financial Management in Web 3.0 105
6.4 Challenges and Regulatory Concerns: Navigating the Web 3.0 Finance Landscape 107
6.5 The Future of Financial Services: Web 3.0 and Beyond 110
Chapter 7: Web 3.0 and the Evolution of Supply Chain Management 112
7.1 Traceability and Transparency: Revolutionizing Supply Chain Management in Web 3.0 113
7.2 Blockchain in Supply Chain: Revolutionizing Transparency and Trust 116

7.3 Smart Contracts for Supply Chain: Streamlining Operations in Web 3.0..119
7.4 Real-World Examples: Web 3.0's Impact on Supply Chain Management 122
7.5 Challenges and Future Trends in Web 3.0 Supply Chain Management 124

Chapter 8: Shaping the Future of Content Publishing in Web 3.0..127
8.1 Decentralized Content Platforms: A Paradigm Shift in Web 3.0 Content Publishing..128
8.2 Censorship Resistance: Empowering Free Expression in Web 3.0 Content Publishing..131
8.3 Content Monetization in Web 3.0: Revolutionizing How Creators Earn...134
8.4 Intellectual Property on the Blockchain: Safeguarding Creative Works in Web 3.0 138
8.5 New Models of Content Distribution: Redefining Access and Ownership in Web 3.0 141

Chapter 9: Navigating the Path to Web 3.0: Challenges and Barriers..144
9.1 Scalability Issues: The Struggle to Expand Web 3.0 ..145
9.2 Regulatory and Legal Challenges: Navigating the Regulatory Landscape of Web 3.0 148
9.3 User Adoption Hurdles: Bridging the Gap to Web 3.0151
9.4 Interoperability and Standards: Bridging the Web 3.0 Divide 154
9.5 Governance in Decentralized Systems: A Key Challenge on the Path to Web 3.0 157

Chapter 10: The Future of Web 3.0: Shaping a Decentralized Digital Landscape 160
10.1 Anticipated Technological Advances: Pioneering the Future of Web 3.0..161

10.2 Industry and Business Transformation: Navigating Web 3.0's Disruptive Wave..165
10.3 The Societal Impact of Web 3.0: Navigating a New Social Order...168
10.4 Preparing for a Decentralized Future: Navigating the Transition to Web 3.0...171
10.5 Conclusion and Call to Action: Shaping the Web 3.0 Future 175
11 Glossary of Terms: Web 3.0 and Decentralized Technologies 178
12 References and Further Reading 182
   12.1 Books..182
   12.2 Online Resources...183
   12.3 Academic Journals and Papers..................................184
   12.4 Forums and Communities 184

Chapter 1: Introduction to Web 3.0

1.1 The Evolution of the Web

The story of Web 3.0 begins with an understanding of the fascinating journey that the World Wide Web has undertaken since its inception. The web, which once comprised static pages and limited interactivity, has evolved through multiple generations, each marked by significant technological advancements and shifts in user interaction. Let's explore this evolution to appreciate how Web 3.0 represents the latest and most transformative phase in the development of the internet.

1.1.1 Web 1.0: The Static Web

The first generation of the web, often referred to as "Web 1.0," emerged in the early 1990s. It was a relatively simple and static environment where web pages served as digital brochures. Information was primarily consumed, and user interaction was limited to clicking hyperlinks to navigate between pages. During this era, websites were rudimentary and focused on providing information rather than facilitating user engagement.

1.1.2 Web 2.0: The Interactive Web

The turn of the millennium ushered in the era of "Web 2.0." This marked a significant shift in the web's character. Web 2.0 was characterized by the emergence of dynamic content and interactive user experiences. Websites became platforms for collaboration, enabling users to contribute content, share opinions, and engage in online communities. Social media, blogs, and user-generated content proliferated. The web became a space where users not only consumed information but also actively participated in its creation.

1.1.3 Web 2.0 Impact on Society

Web 2.0 had a profound impact on society. It redefined communication, connecting people across the globe and enabling instant information sharing. Social networking platforms became an integral part of our daily lives, transforming how we interact with friends, family, and even strangers. Online marketplaces and e-commerce flourished, altering traditional business models. However, Web 2.0 was not without its challenges, notably issues related to data privacy, security, and centralized control.

1.1.4 Web 3.0: The Decentralized Web

Web 3.0, the focus of this book, represents the next chapter in the web's evolution. It transcends the boundaries of Web 2.0 by addressing some of its inherent limitations. The key characteristic of Web 3.0 is decentralization. Unlike its predecessors, Web 3.0 seeks to disperse power, control, and data ownership. It envisions a web where individuals have greater control over their digital identities, data, and online experiences.

In the chapters that follow, we will explore the technologies and concepts that underpin Web 3.0, including blockchain, smart contracts, and decentralized applications (DApps). We'll discuss the implications of this shift in terms of data ownership, security, and trust. Web 3.0 promises to redefine the internet's structure, empowering users and creating a more secure, transparent, and user-centric online environment.

The evolution of the web is an ongoing narrative, and Web 3.0 represents the most exciting and transformative chapter yet. As we delve deeper into the world of decentralized technologies, you'll gain a comprehensive understanding of how these innovations are shaping the future of the internet. This journey is an opportunity to be at the forefront of a new digital era, where individuals and communities regain control of the online landscape.

1.2 The Centralized Web's Limitations

As we venture into the realm of Web 3.0, it's crucial to recognize the inherent limitations of the centralized web, often referred to as Web 2.0. While Web 2.0 has brought about remarkable advancements in terms of user interactivity and content sharing, it has also exposed several challenges that have spurred the need for a more decentralized and user-centric web.

1.2.1 Data Privacy and Ownership

In the centralized web, data privacy has been a recurring concern. The vast troves of personal data collected by tech giants and online platforms have raised questions about who controls this data and how it's used. The centralized nature of Web 2.0 means that data often resides in the hands of a few powerful entities, making it vulnerable to breaches, unauthorized access, and exploitation.

1.2.2 Single Points of Failure

Centralization also gives rise to single points of failure. When a key service or platform experiences downtime or a security breach, it can disrupt the digital lives of millions. We've witnessed instances where outages on major platforms have impacted businesses, communication, and even emergency services, highlighting the fragility of centralized systems.

1.2.3 Censorship and Control

The centralized web allows for the exercise of considerable control over content and users. Governments and corporations can exert influence over what information is disseminated and who can access it. Censorship, whether for political, social, or economic reasons, can limit the free flow of information and stifle open dialogue.

1.2.4 Security Vulnerabilities

Centralized systems are attractive targets for malicious actors. Hacking attempts, data breaches, and cyberattacks are common risks. The accumulation of vast amounts of data in centralized databases creates a lucrative target for cybercriminals.

1.2.5 Lack of User Control

In a centralized web, users have limited control over their digital identities and online experiences. Social media platforms, for example, dictate the terms of engagement, and users often surrender control of their content and data in exchange for access to these platforms.

1.2.6 Trust Deficits

The centralized web relies heavily on trust in intermediaries. Users must trust platform providers to handle their data responsibly and ethically. However, a series of data scandals and breaches have eroded this trust, underscoring the need for more secure and transparent systems.

1.2.7 Web 3.0: A Response to Centralization's Challenges

Web 3.0, with its core principles of decentralization, security, and user empowerment, is positioned as a response to the limitations of the centralized web. The technologies underpinning Web 3.0, such as blockchain, enable data to be distributed across a network of nodes, reducing the risk of data breaches and single points of failure. Smart contracts provide transparent and automated agreements, while decentralized applications (DApps) offer more user-controlled experiences.

In this book, we will explore how Web 3.0 addresses these challenges and leverages decentralization to create a more secure, transparent, and user-centric internet. The decentralized web offers the promise of data ownership, security, and trust in a landscape where individuals and communities are no longer passive consumers but active participants in shaping the digital future.

1.3 The Promise of Web 3.0

Web 3.0 is more than just the next chapter in the evolution of the internet; it's a promise of a fundamental shift in how we experience the digital world. This chapter delves into the profound potential and transformative possibilities that Web 3.0 holds, outlining the key concepts that drive this vision and the impact it can have on individuals, businesses, and society as a whole.

1.3.1 Decentralization

At the heart of Web 3.0 is decentralization. This concept signifies a shift of control and ownership from centralized authorities to a distributed network of users. In a decentralized web, data isn't stored in a single server owned by a corporation; instead, it's distributed across a global network of nodes, making it more secure and resilient. The promise of decentralization extends to various aspects of the web, from content and identity to finance and governance.

1.3.2 Ownership of Data

One of the most compelling promises of Web 3.0 is the ownership of data. In the centralized web, users often surrender control of their personal information and digital identities to tech giants and platforms. In the decentralized web, individuals have greater control over their data, choosing what to share, with whom, and for what purpose. Web 3.0 aims to empower users to monetize their data and protect their privacy.

1.3.3 Security and Trust

Decentralized technologies, such as blockchain, introduce a new level of security and trust to online interactions. Trust is established through transparent, tamper-proof ledgers, and smart contracts automate agreements, reducing the need for intermediaries. Web 3.0 minimizes the risks associated with data breaches, single points of failure, and unauthorized access.

1.3.4 Empowerment through Smart Contracts

Smart contracts are self-executing contracts with the terms of the agreement directly written into code. These contracts enable automated and trustless transactions, reducing the need for traditional legal and financial intermediaries. The promise of Web 3.0 is that individuals and businesses can create, execute, and enforce agreements with unprecedented efficiency and security.

1.3.5 User-Centric Experience

Web 3.0 places individuals at the center of their online experiences. With the proliferation of decentralized applications (DApps), users can access services and content without relying on central platforms. The power to choose how to interact with the digital world and access services becomes a reality, eliminating the walled gardens of the centralized web.

1.3.6 Transparency and Governance

Web 3.0 seeks to introduce transparent and decentralized governance models. In a decentralized internet, users actively participate in decision-making processes through consensus mechanisms. This empowers individuals and communities to have a say in the rules and regulations that govern online spaces.

1.3.7 The Path Forward

As we delve deeper into the chapters of this book, you'll gain a comprehensive understanding of the technologies, principles, and real-world applications that make Web 3.0 a reality. From blockchain and smart contracts to decentralized finance (DeFi) and self-sovereign identity, we will explore how these technologies are disrupting traditional industries and reshaping the digital landscape.

Web 3.0 is a promise of a more inclusive, secure, and user-centric internet. It represents a transformative force that challenges the status quo and empowers individuals to take control of their online experiences. Our journey through the pages that follow is an opportunity to not only understand the promise of Web 3.0 but to actively engage in shaping the future of the internet.

1.4 Key Concepts in Web 3.0

To understand the profound transformation that Web 3.0 brings to the digital landscape, it's essential to grasp the key concepts that underpin this revolutionary shift. These concepts redefine how we perceive, interact with, and benefit from the internet. As we explore the central tenets of Web 3.0, you'll gain insight into the principles that guide its development and the technological innovations that are driving this paradigm change.

1.4.1 Decentralization

Central to the concept of Web 3.0 is decentralization. In the centralized web (Web 2.0), power, control, and data ownership are concentrated in the hands of a few dominant corporations and organizations. Web 3.0 challenges this model by dispersing control and enabling distributed networks. Data is stored across a multitude of nodes rather than on centralized servers. This decentralized approach increases transparency, security, and resilience, as well as empowers individuals to take greater ownership of their digital lives.

1.4.2 Blockchain Technology

Blockchain is the foundational technology of Web 3.0. It is a distributed and immutable ledger that records transactions and data across a network of nodes. This technology ensures transparency, security, and trust by preventing unauthorized alterations. Blockchain's potential applications span beyond cryptocurrencies and extend to supply chain management, voting systems, identity verification, and much more.

1.4.3 Smart Contracts

Smart contracts are self-executing agreements with the terms of the contract directly written into code. These contracts automatically enforce and execute the agreed-upon conditions when predefined triggers are met. They enable trustless transactions and automation of processes, reducing the need for intermediaries. Smart contracts have far-reaching implications in various sectors, including finance, legal, and supply chain management.

1.4.4 Decentralized Applications (DApps)

Decentralized applications, or DApps, are a core component of Web 3.0. Unlike traditional applications that rely on centralized servers, DApps run on decentralized networks, providing users with more control and ownership of their data. These applications offer a wide range of services, from social networks and marketplaces to games and content sharing platforms.

1.4.5 Self-Sovereign Identity

Web 3.0 promotes the concept of self-sovereign identity, where individuals have full control over their digital identities. Users manage and share their identity information as needed, reducing reliance on centralized identity providers and mitigating privacy concerns.

1.4.6 Trustless Transactions

Web 3.0 introduces trustless transactions, meaning that individuals can engage in interactions without needing to trust intermediaries. This trustlessness is achieved through blockchain and smart contracts, which ensure that agreements are executed as programmed without the need for a third party to oversee the process.

1.4.7 Data Ownership and Privacy

Web 3.0 promises to restore ownership and control of personal data to individuals. Users decide how their data is used and can potentially monetize it. This concept addresses the privacy concerns that have arisen in the centralized web.

1.4.8 Transparency and Governance

Decentralization also extends to governance. In Web 3.0, decisions regarding network rules and protocols are made collectively, often through consensus mechanisms. This transparent and community-driven approach empowers users to have a say in the rules that govern their online experiences.

1.4.9 Security and Resilience

The decentralized architecture of Web 3.0 enhances security by reducing the vulnerabilities associated with centralized systems. Data breaches, single points of failure, and malicious activities become less likely due to the distribution of data and control.

1.4.10 The Transformative Power of Web 3.0

Understanding these key concepts is essential as we embark on our journey into the world of Web 3.0 and decentralized technologies. Each of these concepts plays a pivotal role in reshaping the internet and online experiences. As we delve into the subsequent chapters, you'll witness how these concepts come to life in the form of practical applications and real-world use cases, ultimately shaping the future of the internet.

1.5 Web 3.0 Use Cases

Web 3.0 is not just a theoretical concept; it is a reality with a wide array of practical use cases that are already reshaping various industries and domains. These use cases exemplify the transformative potential of Web 3.0, illustrating how decentralized technologies are addressing real-world challenges and opening new opportunities for individuals, businesses, and society. Here are some key use cases that we'll explore in this book:

1.5.1 Decentralized Finance (DeFi)

Decentralized finance, or DeFi, is one of the most prominent and impactful use cases of Web 3.0. DeFi leverages blockchain and smart contracts to create a decentralized financial ecosystem. Users can access a wide range of financial services, including lending, borrowing, trading, and yield farming, without relying on traditional financial institutions. This use case democratizes finance, providing access to financial services for people worldwide.

1.5.2 Digital Identity and Self-Sovereign Identity

Web 3.0 empowers individuals to take control of their digital identities. With self-sovereign identity, users manage their identity information and share it as needed, reducing reliance on centralized identity providers. This has applications in personal data management, online authentication, and identity verification, enhancing privacy and security.

1.5.3 Supply Chain Management

Blockchain technology is revolutionizing supply chain management by providing transparency, traceability, and security. From food safety to luxury goods authentication, blockchain ensures the integrity of products as they move through the supply chain. This use case reduces fraud, counterfeit goods, and inefficiencies.

1.5.4 Content Publishing and Distribution

Web 3.0 is transforming content creation, distribution, and monetization. Content creators can publish their work on decentralized platforms, bypassing traditional media gatekeepers. Smart contracts enable microtransactions, ensuring fair compensation for content producers. This use case challenges traditional media models and empowers creators.

1.5.5 Voting and Governance

Blockchain technology has the potential to revolutionize voting systems and governance. Transparent and tamper-proof ledgers can secure the electoral process, reduce fraud, and increase voter trust. Decentralized governance models enable users to participate in decision-making processes in a transparent and democratic manner.

1.5.6 Intellectual Property and Licensing

Web 3.0 introduces new ways to manage intellectual property and licensing. Artists, writers, and creators can use blockchain to prove ownership and manage royalties automatically through smart contracts. This use case ensures fair compensation and intellectual property protection.

1.5.7 Gaming and Virtual Worlds

The gaming industry is embracing Web 3.0 technologies, creating decentralized gaming platforms and virtual worlds. Gamers can own, trade, and monetize in-game assets through blockchain, opening up new economic opportunities within virtual environments.

1.5.8 Decentralized Social Networks

Web 3.0 challenges traditional social networks by introducing decentralized alternatives. Users can interact on platforms where they have more control over their data and content. These networks prioritize privacy, security, and user ownership.

1.5.9 Healthcare and Medical Records

Web 3.0 offers solutions for secure and interoperable healthcare records. Patients can control their medical data, granting access to healthcare providers on a need-to-know basis. This use case improves data security and healthcare quality.

1.5.10 Legal and Smart Contracts

Smart contracts have applications in legal and contractual matters, automating agreements and reducing the need for intermediaries. They are used in various industries, from real estate to insurance, to streamline processes and increase transparency.

These use cases are just the beginning of the transformative potential of Web 3.0. As we journey through the chapters ahead, we will explore each of these use cases in greater depth, providing insights into the technologies, principles, and real-world applications that make Web 3.0 a game-changer in the digital landscape.

Chapter 2: Blockchain Technology

2.1 The Fundamentals of Blockchain

Blockchain technology lies at the heart of Web 3.0, revolutionizing the way data is stored, shared, and secured. To fully grasp the potential of Web 3.0, it's essential to understand the fundamentals of blockchain, the underlying technology that powers many of the decentralized applications and systems reshaping the digital landscape. In this chapter, we'll delve into the core principles of blockchain and how they enable decentralization and trust.

2.1.1 Distributed Ledger Technology

At its core, a blockchain is a distributed ledger. Traditional ledgers, whether for financial transactions or data storage, are centralized and vulnerable to manipulation or fraud. In contrast, a blockchain is a decentralized ledger distributed across a network of nodes (computers). Every node on the network maintains a copy of the entire blockchain. This distribution ensures transparency and security as all transactions and data entries are visible to all participants.

2.1.2 Blocks and Transactions

A blockchain consists of a series of blocks, each containing a set of transactions. When a transaction is initiated, it is verified by network participants (nodes) and grouped into a block. Once a block reaches a consensus among network nodes, it is added to the blockchain. Each block contains a reference to the previous block, forming a chronological chain of blocks, hence the name "blockchain."

2.1.3 Immutability and Security

One of the most significant advantages of blockchain is its immutability. Once a transaction is added to a block and that block is added to the chain, it becomes nearly impossible to alter or delete the data. This immutability is achieved through cryptographic hashing, which ensures that any change to a block would require consensus from the majority of the network, making it highly secure against unauthorized alterations.

2.1.4 Consensus Mechanisms

Consensus mechanisms are protocols that ensure agreement among network participants on the validity of transactions. Common consensus mechanisms include Proof of Work (PoW) and Proof of Stake (PoS). PoW relies on computational work (mining) to validate transactions, while PoS leverages the ownership of cryptocurrency as collateral to validate transactions. Consensus mechanisms are the backbone of blockchain security and decentralization.

2.1.5 Transparency and Privacy

Blockchain provides transparency by making all transactions and data entries publicly accessible. However, it also allows for privacy through cryptographic techniques. Users can have public addresses for transparency while keeping their real-world identity private. This balance between transparency and privacy is a crucial feature of Web 3.0.

2.1.6 Smart Contracts

Smart contracts are self-executing contracts with the terms of the agreement directly written into code. These contracts automate and enforce agreements when predefined conditions are met. They eliminate the need for intermediaries, reducing the risk of fraud and increasing efficiency in various industries.

2.1.7 Cryptocurrencies

Many blockchains have their native cryptocurrencies, such as Bitcoin and Ethereum. These digital currencies have use cases beyond traditional money. They are integral to blockchain operations, serving as incentives for network participants and powering decentralized applications.

2.1.8 Use Cases

Blockchain technology has a broad range of use cases, from financial services (cryptocurrencies and DeFi) to supply chain management, healthcare, legal processes, and more. Each use case leverages the core features of blockchain, such as transparency, security, and decentralization, to address specific challenges.

Understanding these fundamental principles of blockchain is the first step in grasping the power and potential of Web 3.0. As we progress through this chapter and the subsequent chapters, you'll explore the practical applications and real-world use cases of blockchain, gaining a deeper appreciation for how this technology is reshaping our digital future.

2.2 Cryptography and Security

Cryptography forms the bedrock of security in blockchain technology. It provides the means to protect data, secure transactions, and maintain the integrity of the decentralized ledger. In this chapter, we'll delve into the role of cryptography and its critical importance in blockchain security.

2.2.1 Secure Data Transmission

Blockchain transactions involve sensitive data, and it's vital to protect this information during transmission. Cryptographic techniques like Secure Sockets Layer (SSL) and Transport Layer Security (TLS) encrypt data as it travels between users and nodes. This encryption ensures that data remains confidential and tamper-proof.

2.2.2 Digital Signatures

Digital signatures are at the core of blockchain security. They provide a way for participants to prove the authenticity of their transactions and messages. When a user initiates a transaction, they sign it with their private key, creating a digital signature. Others can verify the signature using the user's public key, confirming the transaction's origin and integrity.

2.2.3 Hash Functions

Hash functions play a vital role in blockchain security. These functions take an input (data) and produce a fixed-size string of characters, the hash. Hashes are unique to the input, and even a small change in the input data results in a significantly different hash. This property makes hashes ideal for verifying data integrity. Hashes are used to verify the integrity of blocks in the blockchain and secure the connections between blocks through their reference to the previous block's hash.

2.2.4 Public and Private Keys

Public and private key pairs are the cornerstone of blockchain security. Each user or node in the network has a unique pair. The public key is used to verify digital signatures, while the private key is kept secret and used to create those signatures. The asymmetric nature of this system ensures that even if the public key is known, it is computationally infeasible to derive the private key.

2.2.5 Encryption and Decryption

Cryptography is also used to encrypt and decrypt data stored on the blockchain. For instance, in systems like Ethereum, smart contract code and data can be encrypted to maintain privacy. Decryption can only occur with the private keys of the authorized users.

2.2.6 Consensus Mechanisms

Consensus mechanisms, such as Proof of Work (PoW) and Proof of Stake (PoS), rely on cryptographic principles to secure the network. PoW requires participants to perform complex cryptographic puzzles to validate transactions, while PoS uses ownership of cryptocurrency as collateral. These mechanisms ensure that malicious actors cannot easily manipulate the network.

2.2.7 Privacy Coins and Confidential Transactions

Privacy-focused cryptocurrencies and protocols, like Monero and Zcash, incorporate advanced cryptographic techniques to provide anonymous and confidential transactions. Zero-knowledge proofs and ring signatures are examples of cryptographic tools used to obscure transaction details while maintaining security.

2.2.8 Quantum-Resistant Cryptography

The advent of quantum computing poses a potential threat to current cryptographic systems. As quantum computers could potentially break existing encryption methods, the development of quantum-resistant cryptography is an ongoing field, ensuring that blockchain systems remain secure in the face of evolving threats.

2.2.9 Security in a Decentralized World

Cryptography is the linchpin of security in the blockchain and Web 3.0 ecosystem. It enables secure data transmission, identity verification, and data integrity. As we explore the subsequent chapters, you'll witness how cryptography, combined with other blockchain technologies, ensures the robust security of decentralized applications and systems, reinforcing the promise of Web 3.0 as a safer and more trustworthy digital frontier.

2.3 Blockchain Consensus Mechanisms

Blockchain technology's decentralization and security rely heavily on consensus mechanisms. These are protocols that ensure agreement among network participants on the validity of transactions and the state of the distributed ledger. Understanding the various consensus mechanisms is crucial in comprehending the inner workings of blockchain technology. In this chapter, we'll explore some of the most common consensus mechanisms and their impact on the Web 3.0 landscape.

2.3.1 Proof of Work (PoW)

Proof of Work is one of the earliest and most well-known consensus mechanisms, famously used in Bitcoin. In a PoW system, participants (miners) compete to solve complex mathematical puzzles. The first miner to solve the puzzle gets to validate a block of transactions and adds it to the blockchain. PoW ensures network security by making it computationally expensive to manipulate the blockchain. However, it is energy-intensive and can lead to centralization in mining due to the concentration of resources.

2.3.2 Proof of Stake (PoS)

Proof of Stake is an alternative to PoW. In a PoS system, validators (participants with a stake in the network) are chosen to create and validate blocks based on the amount of cryptocurrency they hold and are willing to "stake" as collateral. PoS is more energy-efficient compared to PoW, as it doesn't rely on resource-intensive mining. It also reduces the risk of centralization since validators are chosen based on their stake.

2.3.3 Delegated Proof of Stake (DPoS)

Delegated Proof of Stake is a variation of PoS where stakeholders vote for a limited number of delegates or "witnesses" who have the authority to validate transactions and create blocks. DPoS aims to improve scalability and consensus speed while maintaining decentralization. It is often used in platforms like EOS and BitShares.

2.3.4 Proof of Authority (PoA)

Proof of Authority is a consensus mechanism where validators are known and trusted entities. They are given the authority to validate transactions based on their reputation, and in some cases, they may be held accountable for their actions. PoA is known for its high throughput and is commonly used in permissioned or private blockchains.

2.3.5 Proof of Space and Time (PoST)

Proof of Space and Time is a novel consensus mechanism that leverages unused storage space on a user's device. Miners prove they have dedicated space and kept it unused for a specified time. PoST is more energy-efficient than PoW and is considered environmentally friendly.

2.3.6 Byzantine Fault Tolerance (BFT)

Byzantine Fault Tolerance is a consensus mechanism designed to work efficiently in systems where malicious actors can be present. It relies on a threshold of validators who must agree on the state of the network. BFT ensures security against adversarial nodes by requiring consensus among a significant portion of honest validators.

2.3.7 Practical Byzantine Fault Tolerance (PBFT)

Practical Byzantine Fault Tolerance is a specific implementation of BFT, commonly used in permissioned blockchain networks. It ensures consensus among a set of known and trusted nodes. PBFT excels in systems where network participants are known entities and trust is paramount.

2.3.8 Tendermint

Tendermint is a consensus mechanism and platform that utilizes Byzantine Fault Tolerance. It is used in various blockchain projects, including the Cosmos network. Tendermint aims to provide fast and secure consensus, suitable for a wide range of applications.

Understanding these consensus mechanisms is essential to appreciate the diversity of approaches in the blockchain space. Each mechanism offers a unique set of features and trade-offs, enabling blockchain systems to cater to different use cases and align with the principles of Web 3.0, which emphasize decentralization, security, and efficiency. As we progress through the chapters, you'll explore how these mechanisms are applied in practical scenarios and contribute to the decentralized technologies shaping Web 3.0.

2.4 Smart Contracts: The Digital Backbone of Web 3.0

Smart contracts are the digital equivalent of traditional legal contracts, but with a crucial difference – they are self-executing and self-enforcing. These contracts are at the heart of Web 3.0, transforming the way agreements are made, validated, and executed. In this chapter, we'll explore the concept of smart contracts, their underlying technology, and their significant impact on decentralized technologies.

2.4.1 The Concept of Smart Contracts

Smart contracts are software programs that automatically execute, enforce, or facilitate the terms of an agreement when predefined conditions are met. These contracts run on blockchain platforms, making them transparent, tamper-proof, and trustless. Smart contracts can represent a wide range of agreements, from financial transactions and legal agreements to supply chain management and decentralized applications.

2.4.2 Key Components of Smart Contracts

Smart contracts consist of several key components:

- **Code**: The logic of the contract is written in code, often using programming languages like Solidity (for Ethereum), making it programmable and customizable.

- **Data**: Smart contracts can hold and manipulate data, creating a self-contained environment for agreement execution.

- **Addresses**: Smart contracts are associated with unique addresses on the blockchain, allowing them to be easily identified and interacted with.

- **Transactions**: The execution of a smart contract involves transactions on the blockchain, each of which triggers specific actions within the contract.

2.4.3 Automation and Trustlessness

One of the primary advantages of smart contracts is automation. Once the contract is deployed on the blockchain, it operates without the need for intermediaries. The code and the consensus mechanism of the blockchain ensure that the contract's execution is trustless, meaning that it doesn't rely on trust between parties. This trustlessness reduces the risk of fraud and minimizes the need for third-party verification.

2.4.4 Use Cases of Smart Contracts

Smart contracts have diverse use cases:

- **Financial Services**: They can automate lending, borrowing, and trading, enabling decentralized finance (DeFi) platforms.

- **Supply Chain Management**: Smart contracts track the movement of goods, ensuring transparency and reducing fraud in the supply chain.

- **Legal and Governance**: They can be used for notarization, voting, and governance decisions, eliminating the need for manual intervention.

- **Content Publishing**: Smart contracts enable content creators to automate royalty payments and monetize their work transparently.

- **Identity Verification**: They provide secure and decentralized identity verification services.

2.4.5 Challenges and Limitations

While smart contracts offer tremendous potential, they are not without challenges. They are irreversible, which means that mistakes in code or unintended consequences can be costly. Security vulnerabilities, such as those leading to hacks or exploits, are significant concerns. Scalability issues, where the execution of a large number of contracts on the blockchain can lead to congestion, are also being addressed.

2.4.6 The Future of Smart Contracts

As Web 3.0 evolves, smart contracts will play an increasingly pivotal role in reshaping how agreements are made and executed. Advancements in technology, tools, and best practices are continually improving the security, efficiency, and usability of smart contracts. Their impact extends beyond the financial sector to governance, legal processes, and decentralized applications, contributing to a more automated, secure, and decentralized digital future.

In the subsequent chapters, we will dive deeper into practical applications of smart contracts and explore the tools and platforms that make them accessible to developers and users, ultimately shaping the decentralized technologies of Web 3.0.

2.5 Use Cases for Blockchain

Blockchain technology is a versatile and transformative force with applications across various industries and sectors. Its fundamental characteristics, such as decentralization, transparency, and security, have opened up a wide array of use cases, many of which are poised to shape the future of Web 3.0. In this chapter, we will explore some prominent use cases for blockchain technology.

2.5.1 Cryptocurrencies and Digital Assets

Cryptocurrencies like Bitcoin, Ethereum, and a multitude of others are perhaps the most well-known use case for blockchain. They provide a decentralized and secure means of conducting digital transactions, making them an alternative to traditional currencies. In addition to being a medium of exchange, blockchain technology enables the creation and management of various digital assets and tokens.

2.5.2 Decentralized Finance (DeFi)

DeFi is a rapidly growing sector that leverages blockchain to recreate traditional financial services, such as lending, borrowing, trading, and asset management, in a decentralized and open manner. DeFi platforms use smart contracts to automate financial agreements, reducing the need for intermediaries and increasing financial inclusion.

2.5.3 Supply Chain Management

Blockchain is being adopted to increase transparency and traceability in supply chains. It enables the tracking of products and materials from their origin to the end user. This use case is especially critical in industries like food, pharmaceuticals, and luxury goods to ensure quality, authenticity, and safety.

2.5.4 Digital Identity and Self-Sovereign Identity

Blockchain provides a foundation for secure and self-sovereign digital identities. Users can manage their identity and personal data, only sharing information when necessary. This approach improves privacy and security in identity management, reducing reliance on centralized identity providers.

2.5.5 Voting and Governance

Blockchain offers a secure and transparent solution for voting systems and governance processes. It can help prevent fraud and manipulation in elections while enhancing the transparency and integrity of decision-making in organizations and communities.

2.5.6 Intellectual Property and Licensing

Blockchain provides artists, writers, and creators with a secure platform to manage their intellectual property. Through blockchain-based solutions, creators can prove ownership, track usage, and automatically receive royalties for their work.

2.5.7 Healthcare and Medical Records

Blockchain technology ensures the security and interoperability of healthcare records. Patients can control access to their medical data, granting permission only to authorized healthcare providers. This use case enhances data security and streamlines healthcare processes.

2.5.8 Legal and Smart Contracts

Smart contracts on blockchain platforms are automating legal agreements and contractual processes. These self-executing contracts streamline operations in various industries, from real estate to insurance, by eliminating intermediaries and automating the execution of agreements.

2.5.9 Gaming and Virtual Worlds

Blockchain has disrupted the gaming industry by enabling the ownership, trading, and monetization of in-game assets. Players can have true ownership of their digital items, opening new economic opportunities within virtual environments.

2.5.10 Content Publishing and Distribution

Blockchain-based platforms empower content creators to publish their work without intermediaries. Smart contracts ensure fair compensation and transparent revenue-sharing mechanisms for content creators, reducing the influence of traditional media gatekeepers.

2.5.11 Decentralized Social Networks

Blockchain has given rise to decentralized alternatives to traditional social networks. These networks prioritize user data privacy and ownership, providing more control and transparency to users.

2.5.12 Legal Notarization

Blockchain can be used to create immutable and timestamped records for legal notarization. This technology enhances the security and reliability of legal documents.

These use cases exemplify the versatility and potential of blockchain technology in the Web 3.0 landscape. As we proceed through this chapter and the following chapters, we will delve deeper into each of these use cases, exploring the underlying technology, real-world applications, and the ways they contribute to a more decentralized, secure, and efficient digital future.

Chapter 3: Decentralized Applications (DApps)

The evolution of the internet has seen it transition from a static information resource to an interactive platform that has revolutionized nearly every aspect of our lives. However, this evolution is far from complete. Web 3.0, the next phase of the internet's development, is marked by an exciting shift towards decentralization, security, and user empowerment. At the forefront of this transformation are Decentralized Applications, or DApps.

In this chapter, we will embark on a journey through the world of DApps, exploring their nature, significance, and their profound impact on the way we interact, transact, and create on the web. As we delve deeper into this topic, we will uncover the core principles that underpin DApps, their advantages over traditional applications, and the diverse array of use cases that they are poised to disrupt.

3.1 The Birth of DApps

The emergence of Decentralized Applications, or DApps, marks a pivotal moment in the evolution of the internet. This shift towards decentralization is reshaping the way we envision, build, and interact with applications on the web. To truly understand the significance of DApps in the context of Web 3.0, it's essential to explore their origins and the key events that led to their birth.

3.1.1 The Blockchain Revolution

The inception of DApps is intrinsically tied to the rise of blockchain technology. Blockchain, first introduced through Bitcoin, showcased the potential for decentralized networks and trustless transactions. This breakthrough opened the door to the creation of applications that could operate without centralized control, intermediaries, or the need for user trust.

3.1.2 Bitcoin: The Proto-DApp

Bitcoin, often considered the proto-DApp, was the first application to demonstrate the potential of decentralized technology. It enabled peer-to-peer electronic cash transactions without relying on banks or financial institutions. The Bitcoin blockchain acted as a decentralized ledger, recording all transactions transparently and securely. This model set the stage for the development of DApps in various domains.

3.1.3 Ethereum and the Smart Contract Revolution

Ethereum, launched in 2015 by Vitalik Buterin and others, introduced the concept of smart contracts to the world. Smart contracts are self-executing agreements with code that automates the execution of contract terms when specific conditions are met. Ethereum's blockchain allowed developers to build DApps on its platform, leveraging smart contracts to create a wide range of decentralized applications.

3.1.4 The Crowdfunding Boom

Ethereum's introduction came with an innovative way to raise funds for DApp development – Initial Coin Offerings (ICOs). These crowdfunding mechanisms allowed developers to secure capital by offering tokens that represented future use within their DApps. This approach kick-started the development of countless DApps in various domains.

3.1.5 The DApp Ecosystem Expands

With the Ethereum platform as a foundation, the DApp ecosystem expanded rapidly. Projects emerged in domains such as decentralized finance (DeFi), supply chain management, content publishing, gaming, identity verification, and more. Each of these DApps aimed to provide a decentralized alternative to traditional centralized systems.

3.1.6 Open Source Collaboration

Many DApps are developed as open-source projects, fostering collaboration among developers and the wider community. This open and collaborative nature contributes to innovation, security, and the development of a diverse DApp ecosystem.

3.1.7 The Advent of Token Standards

Ethereum introduced the ERC-20 token standard, which defined a common interface for fungible tokens on the blockchain. This standardization made it easier for DApps to integrate and exchange tokens. Subsequent token standards, like ERC-721 (for non-fungible tokens), further expanded DApp capabilities.

3.1.8 DApps in a Maturing Web 3.0 Landscape

As the DApp landscape continues to evolve, it has matured into a powerful force in Web 3.0. DApps offer an alternative paradigm, one where data, control, and trust are returned to users. With blockchain technology as the backbone, DApps are challenging centralized systems, forging a path toward a more decentralized, secure, and transparent internet.

The birth of DApps, catalyzed by the blockchain revolution and Ethereum's pioneering work, has set in motion a profound transformation of how we build, use, and interact with digital applications. As we delve further into the world of DApps in this chapter, we will explore their underlying technology, diverse use cases, and the challenges they face. These applications are at the forefront of the Web 3.0 movement, championing the values of decentralization and user empowerment.

3.2 How DApps Work: The Mechanics of Decentralized Applications

Decentralized Applications, or DApps, are a groundbreaking innovation in the realm of software development, disrupting the traditional model of centralized applications. They harness the power of blockchain technology to create transparent, trustless, and decentralized systems. In this section, we'll explore the mechanics of how DApps work and the underlying technology that enables their functionality.

3.2.1 Blockchain as the Foundation

The cornerstone of DApps is the blockchain. A blockchain is a distributed and immutable ledger that records all transactions across a network of nodes. It operates on the principles of decentralization, cryptographic security, and consensus mechanisms, making it resistant to tampering and fraud. Blockchain technology ensures the trustworthiness and transparency of DApps.

3.2.2 Smart Contracts: The Heart of DApps

At the core of many DApps are smart contracts. Smart contracts are self-executing code with predefined rules and conditions. They run on the blockchain and automate various functions, eliminating the need for intermediaries. Smart contracts are integral to DApps because they facilitate trustless and transparent interactions.

3.2.3 The DApp Architecture

The architecture of a DApp is distinctive and comprises several key components:

- **Frontend**: The user interface of the DApp, often built using familiar web technologies like HTML, CSS, and JavaScript. The frontend interacts with the blockchain and smart contracts through APIs.

- **Backend**: In a traditional application, the backend logic is hosted on centralized servers. In DApps, the backend logic is often executed by smart contracts on the blockchain, making it decentralized and transparent.

- **Blockchain**: The blockchain serves as the database and ledger for the DApp. It records all transactions, data, and the execution of smart contracts. This data is stored across a distributed network of nodes.

- **Consensus Mechanism**: The blockchain relies on a consensus mechanism, such as Proof of Work (PoW) or Proof of Stake (PoS), to validate and confirm transactions. This ensures that the ledger remains tamper-proof.

3.2.4 DApp Interactions

When a user interacts with a DApp, the following process occurs:

- **User Action**: A user initiates an action through the DApp's frontend, such as making a transaction, creating content, or participating in a game.

- **Transaction Creation**: The DApp creates a transaction request, which is sent to the blockchain network.

- **Smart Contract Execution**: The smart contract responsible for processing the user's request is executed on the blockchain. The smart contract validates the request and ensures that the predefined conditions are met.

- **Consensus and Confirmation**: The blockchain's consensus mechanism confirms the transaction's validity and records it on the ledger. This process often involves miners or validators who secure the network and maintain the blockchain.

- **User Feedback**: The DApp's frontend is updated to reflect the transaction's status. Users can view the results of their action on the DApp's interface.

3.2.5 Advantages of DApps

DApps offer a range of advantages over traditional applications:

- **Security**: The decentralized nature of DApps reduces the risk of data breaches and hacks. Data is secured through cryptography and the blockchain's immutability.

- **Transparency**: Users can inspect the blockchain to verify transactions, smart contract logic, and data, enhancing trust.

- **Trustlessness**: DApps eliminate the need for trust between users and intermediaries, as the blockchain enforces agreements and transactions.

- **Ownership**: Users have greater control and ownership of their data, digital assets, and interactions.

- **Censorship Resistance**: DApps are less susceptible to censorship, making them ideal for applications requiring free and open access to information.

As we proceed through this chapter, we will explore real-world examples of DApps in various domains, from finance to supply chain management and social networks. We will also address the challenges and limitations of DApps and discuss their role in shaping the future of the internet in the era of Web 3.0.

3.3 Types of DApps: Pioneering Decentralized Solutions

Decentralized Applications, or DApps, are not confined to a single domain; their versatility spans a wide spectrum of use cases. These innovative applications leverage blockchain technology to usher in a new era of transparency, trustlessness, and decentralization. In this section, we will explore the various types of DApps and their significant contributions to Web 3.0.

3.3.1 Finance and Decentralized Finance (DeFi) DApps

DeFi DApps have redefined the financial landscape by providing open, decentralized alternatives to traditional financial services. These applications offer features like lending, borrowing, trading, and asset management without the need for intermediaries. DeFi DApps often incorporate stablecoins, liquidity pools, and yield farming to create a vibrant and user-centric financial ecosystem.

3.3.2 Supply Chain Management DApps

Supply chain management DApps focus on enhancing transparency, traceability, and efficiency in supply chains. They leverage blockchain's immutability to record the journey of products and materials from source to destination. These DApps are invaluable in industries such as food, pharmaceuticals, and luxury goods to ensure authenticity, quality, and safety.

3.3.3 Content Publishing and Social Media DApps

Content publishing and social media DApps aim to provide censorship-resistant and user-owned platforms for content creators. Users have greater control over their data and interactions, reducing the influence of centralized content platforms. This type of DApp fosters open dialogue and free expression.

3.3.4 Gaming and Virtual Worlds DApps

Gaming DApps have revolutionized the gaming industry by enabling true ownership of in-game assets. These DApps use non-fungible tokens (NFTs) to represent unique in-game items that players can buy, sell, and trade. Virtual worlds within DApps allow players to participate in economies that mirror real-world markets.

3.3.5 Identity Verification DApps

Identity verification DApps provide secure and self-sovereign digital identity solutions. Users can control access to their personal data and identity information, sharing it only when necessary. This type of DApp enhances data privacy and security.

3.3.6 Governance DApps

Governance DApps facilitate transparent and decentralized decision-making processes. They enable voting, proposal creation, and governance of organizations, communities, and protocols. These applications are valuable for projects seeking community involvement and consensus.

3.3.7 Legal and Notarization DApps

Legal and notarization DApps leverage blockchain's immutability to create timestamped records for legal documents and agreements. These DApps enhance the security and reliability of legal processes and notarization.

3.3.8 Healthcare and Medical Records DApps

Healthcare and medical records DApps provide secure and interoperable solutions for managing patient data. Patients can control who accesses their medical information, ensuring privacy and data security.

3.3.9 Real Estate DApps

Real estate DApps are changing how property transactions are conducted. They offer streamlined processes for buying, selling, and managing real estate through smart contracts, reducing the need for intermediaries.

3.3.10 Intellectual Property and Licensing DApps

Intellectual property and licensing DApps empower creators to manage their intellectual property. These DApps help artists, writers, and content creators prove ownership, track usage, and receive royalties for their work.

3.3.11 Charity and Donation DApps

Charity and donation DApps provide transparent and traceable methods for contributing to charitable causes. Users can track donations and ensure funds reach their intended recipients.

These are just a few examples of the diverse DApp landscape, each serving a unique purpose and bringing the principles of decentralization, transparency, and user empowerment to their respective domains. As we progress through this chapter, we will delve deeper into some of these DApp types, exploring their technology, real-world applications, and the impact they are making in their industries. DApps are at the forefront of Web 3.0, driving a movement towards a more decentralized, secure, and user-centric internet.

3.4 Benefits and Challenges of DApps

Decentralized Applications (DApps) represent a paradigm shift in software development, promising numerous benefits while also presenting unique challenges. Understanding both the advantages and hurdles is crucial for appreciating the significance of DApps in the context of Web 3.0.

3.4.1 Benefits of DApps

1. **Decentralization**: DApps operate on decentralized networks, reducing the risk of single points of failure. This decentralization fosters trustlessness and transparency, eliminating the need for intermediaries.

2. **Security**: Blockchain technology and cryptographic mechanisms enhance the security of DApps. The immutable nature of the blockchain makes it resistant to data breaches and hacks.

3. **Transparency**: DApps record all transactions on the blockchain, providing users with full transparency. Users can verify the integrity of data, transactions, and smart contract logic.

4. **Ownership and Control**: DApp users have greater control over their data and digital assets. They can interact with DApps without surrendering control to third-party service providers.

5. **Censorship Resistance**: DApps are less susceptible to censorship, making them ideal for applications that require open access to information, free expression, and resistance to censorship.

6. **Trustless Transactions**: Smart contracts embedded in DApps ensure that agreements are executed automatically when conditions are met. This trustless approach eliminates the need for trust between parties.

7. **Open Source Collaboration**: Many DApps are developed as open-source projects, encouraging collaboration and innovation within the developer community.

8. **Token Integration**: DApps often incorporate tokens, enabling various functionalities within the ecosystem. Users can earn, trade, or use tokens for various purposes within the DApp.

9. **Innovation**: DApps are at the forefront of technological innovation, exploring new possibilities in industries like finance, supply chain, and social media.

3.4.2 Challenges of DApps:

1. **Scalability**: Some DApps face challenges in scaling to accommodate a large number of users and transactions. Blockchain networks must address scalability concerns to support widespread adoption.

2. **Usability**: The user experience of DApps can be less intuitive compared to centralized applications. Improving the user interface and experience is a constant challenge.

3. **Regulatory Compliance**: DApps operating in financial, legal, or highly regulated domains face complex regulatory challenges. Complying with legal frameworks while maintaining decentralization is a delicate balance.

4. **Interoperability**: Different blockchain platforms and DApps often use incompatible technologies. Achieving interoperability and data exchange between DApps is an ongoing challenge.

5. **Token Volatility**: The value of tokens used in DApps can be highly volatile, impacting the user experience and adoption.

6. **Smart Contract Security**: Vulnerabilities in smart contracts can lead to exploits and security breaches. Auditing and securing smart contracts is essential.

7. **Adoption and Network Effects**: DApps often face the chicken-and-egg problem of adoption. A critical mass of users and participants is required to realize the full potential of DApps.

8. **Costs and Energy Consumption**: Some blockchain networks, like those using Proof of Work (PoW), consume significant energy and incur high operational costs.

9. **Data Privacy**: While blockchain offers transparency, it can pose challenges for data privacy, especially in applications requiring confidentiality.

10. **User Support**: DApps may lack customer support, as they operate without centralized entities. This can be a drawback for some users.

Understanding the benefits and challenges of DApps is essential for developers, users, and stakeholders alike. Overcoming these challenges is vital to realize the full potential of DApps and their role in shaping the future of the internet in the Web 3.0 era. As we continue exploring DApps in this chapter, we will delve into real-world examples and the impact they are making in various industries.

3.5 Real-World DApp Examples

Decentralized Applications (DApps) have already left a significant mark in various industries by offering innovative solutions that challenge centralized systems. In this section, we will explore real-world DApp examples, highlighting how they are transforming their respective domains and contributing to the ongoing shift toward Web 3.0.

- **Uniswap** (DeFi - Finance): Uniswap is a decentralized exchange protocol built on Ethereum. It enables users to swap various cryptocurrencies without the need for a traditional exchange. Uniswap's automated market maker mechanism and liquidity pools have revolutionized the decentralized finance (DeFi) space, providing users with efficient and decentralized trading options.

- **Aave** (DeFi - Finance): Aave is a decentralized lending and borrowing platform that allows users to lend and borrow cryptocurrencies without intermediaries. Users can earn interest on deposited assets while maintaining control of their funds. Aave has been a key player in the DeFi lending sector.

- **CryptoKitties** (Gaming - Collectibles): CryptoKitties is a blockchain-based game that allows users to collect, breed, and trade digital cats. Each CryptoKitty is represented by a non-fungible token (NFT), making them unique and tradable. This DApp showcases the potential of blockchain in the gaming and collectibles industry.

- **Ethereum Name Service (ENS)** (Identity - Domain): ENS is a decentralized domain name system built on Ethereum. It replaces traditional domain registrars with smart contracts, allowing users to own and manage domain names directly on the blockchain. ENS has introduced a new approach to internet identity and domain management.

- **Audius** (Music - Content): Audius is a decentralized music streaming platform that empowers artists to publish, share, and monetize their music without intermediaries. Audius uses blockchain technology to ensure fair compensation for artists and transparent royalty distribution.

- **Immutable X** (Gaming - NFTs): Immutable X is a Layer-2 scaling solution for Ethereum that specializes in trading and owning NFTs. It offers a gas-free and environmentally friendly way to trade NFTs while retaining the security and decentralization of the Ethereum blockchain.

- **Filecoin** (Storage - Decentralized Storage): Filecoin is a decentralized storage network that allows users to rent out their unused storage space or store data in a secure, decentralized manner. It aims to create a more efficient and censorship-resistant data storage solution.

- **Celo** (Finance - Payments): Celo is a blockchain platform that focuses on making financial tools accessible to anyone with a mobile phone. It facilitates cross-border payments and stablecoin transactions, promoting financial inclusion in underserved regions.

- **Decentraland** (Gaming - Virtual Worlds): Decentraland is a virtual reality platform built on Ethereum. Users can purchase, develop, and sell virtual real estate parcels using the platform's native cryptocurrency. This DApp brings the concept of virtual worlds and digital ownership to life.

- **Brave** (Web Browsing - Privacy): The Brave browser is built around the Basic Attention Token (BAT), which rewards users for viewing ads and content. It offers enhanced privacy and allows users to have more control over their data and online experience.

These real-world DApp examples showcase the diversity of applications enabled by blockchain technology. They are redefining finance, gaming, identity, content sharing, and many other industries, offering users transparency, control, and innovative experiences. As Web 3.0 continues to evolve, DApps are at the forefront of shaping the internet of the future.

Chapter 4: The Decentralized Internet - Navigating the Web 3.0 Landscape

The internet has come a long way since its inception, evolving from a simple network of computers to a sprawling global ecosystem that influences every aspect of our lives. Web 3.0, often referred to as the decentralized internet, is the next phase in this remarkable journey. It is a transformative vision that challenges the centralized structure of the current web, introducing a new era of decentralization, trust, and transparency.

In this chapter, we will embark on a journey through the landscape of the decentralized internet, Web 3.0. We will explore the fundamental principles, technologies, and applications that underpin this paradigm shift and examine how it is poised to reshape the way we access information, conduct transactions, and interact with the digital world.

Web 3.0 envisions a digital realm where centralized control, single points of failure, and data monopolies give way to a distributed, open, and user-centric internet. At its core, it leverages groundbreaking technologies like blockchain and decentralized applications (DApps) to empower individuals and organizations, enabling them to take control of their digital presence and interactions.

As we delve into the chapters ahead, we will uncover the promise and potential of Web 3.0, exploring how it is redefining finance, identity, content creation, and countless other domains. We will also confront the challenges and obstacles that lie in the path of widespread adoption, acknowledging the complexities of regulatory compliance, scalability, and usability.

Our journey through the decentralized internet is a voyage of discovery, offering insights into the transformative impact of blockchain, DApps, and decentralized technologies. It is an exploration of the tools and platforms that are already reshaping industries and influencing the way we perceive and engage with the digital world.

Web 3.0 is not merely a concept; it is a living, breathing movement that invites us to reimagine the internet as a decentralized, transparent, and user-focused ecosystem. Together, we will navigate the ever-expanding frontiers of the decentralized internet, uncovering the potential for a more equitable, open, and user-empowered digital future. Welcome to the decentralized internet, where Web 3.0 is shaping a new digital landscape.

4.1 Web 3.0 and Internet Decentralization: A Paradigm Shift

The internet, as we know it today, has been instrumental in connecting the world, sharing information, and transforming various aspects of society. However, it has not been without its challenges. The centralization of power, control, and data has raised concerns about privacy, security, and equitable access. In response to these limitations, Web 3.0 is emerging as a powerful and transformative force, reimagining the internet as a decentralized ecosystem.

4.1.1 Understanding Web 3.0:

Web 3.0, often referred to as the decentralized internet, represents the next evolutionary phase of the World Wide Web. It introduces a fundamental shift from the centralized model of Web 2.0, where tech giants and intermediaries dominate, to a decentralized model that prioritizes user empowerment, security, and trustlessness.

At the heart of Web 3.0 are revolutionary technologies, with blockchain as a cornerstone. Blockchain's immutability, transparency, and trustless nature have opened the door to decentralized applications (DApps) and smart contracts. These technologies enable users to interact, transact, and create content on a secure, tamper-proof, and transparent platform.

4.1.2 Key Elements of Internet Decentralization:

1. **Blockchain Technology**: The foundation of Web 3.0, blockchain technology ensures data integrity and security by distributing information across a global network of nodes. This immutability and transparency reduce the risk of data manipulation or hacking.

2. **Decentralized Applications (DApps)**: DApps are software applications that operate on blockchain networks rather than centralized servers. They provide services while maintaining user control over data and transactions.

3. **Smart Contracts**: Self-executing contracts, or smart contracts, automate and enforce agreements without the need for intermediaries. They enable trustless transactions and have applications beyond finance, including legal and supply chain management.

4. **Tokenization**: Tokenization is the representation of digital or physical assets as tokens on a blockchain. This enables the creation of unique, tradable assets like non-fungible tokens (NFTs) and security tokens.

5. **Peer-to-Peer Networks**: The decentralized internet relies on peer-to-peer (P2P) networks for communication and data sharing, reducing reliance on centralized servers.

4.1.3 Advantages of Web 3.0:

- **Security**: Blockchain's immutability and encryption enhance data security.
- **Transparency**: Transparent and auditable transactions build trust.
- **User Control**: Users maintain control over their data, digital assets, and online identity.
- **Censorship Resistance**: Content and transactions are resistant to censorship.
- **Trustless Transactions**: Users can engage in transactions without trust in a third party.

4.1.4 Challenges and Complexities:

- **Scalability**: Scalability issues must be addressed to accommodate a global user base.
- **Regulatory Compliance**: Adhering to regulations while preserving decentralization is a delicate balance.

- **Usability**: User-friendly interfaces and experiences are crucial for adoption.
- **Interoperability**: Ensuring compatibility between different blockchain networks is a challenge.

As we journey through the chapters of this book, we will explore the decentralized internet's many facets, from decentralized finance (DeFi) and identity management to gaming and content creation. The decentralized internet isn't just a concept; it's a movement, offering new opportunities for a more open, user-centric, and equitable digital future. It is a revolution that redefines how we interact with the online world, and its impact is already palpable across various domains. Welcome to the era of Web 3.0 and the decentralized internet.

4.2 Decentralized File Storage: Empowering Data Ownership

One of the fundamental challenges of the centralized internet is the way data is stored and controlled. Users often surrender their data to centralized entities, which raises concerns about privacy, security, and data ownership. In the era of Web 3.0, decentralized file storage solutions are emerging as a powerful means to address these concerns, putting control back into the hands of users.

4.2.1 The Shift to Decentralized File Storage

Decentralized file storage is a core component of Web 3.0's vision for a more user-centric internet. Unlike traditional cloud storage systems, where data is stored on centralized servers controlled by corporations, decentralized file storage leverages blockchain and peer-to-peer (P2P) technologies to distribute data across a network of nodes.

4.2.2 Key Elements of Decentralized File Storage

1. **Blockchain Integration**: Many decentralized file storage systems utilize blockchain technology to manage and secure data. Blockchain ensures the integrity and immutability of stored files.

2. **Peer-to-Peer Networks**: P2P networks enable users to store and access data directly from other users' devices, eliminating the need for centralized servers.

3. **Incentive Mechanisms**: Incentives, often in the form of cryptocurrency rewards, encourage users to share their storage space and contribute to the network.

4.2.3 Advantages of Decentralized File Storage

- **Data Ownership**: Users retain ownership and control of their data, deciding who can access and use it.

- **Privacy**: Decentralized storage systems enhance data privacy by reducing the risk of data breaches and unauthorized access.
- **Security**: Blockchain's encryption and immutability enhance data security, reducing the risk of data manipulation or loss.
- **Censorship Resistance**: Data stored in a decentralized network is resistant to censorship, ensuring open access to information.

4.2.4 Real-World Applications

1. **Filecoin**: Filecoin is a decentralized storage network that incentivizes users to rent out their unused storage space in exchange for cryptocurrency. It offers secure and censorship-resistant storage for various data types.

2. **IPFS (InterPlanetary File System)**: IPFS is a protocol and network designed to create a content-addressable, peer-to-peer method of storing and sharing hypermedia in a distributed file system. It underpins various decentralized applications and services.

3. **Sia**: Sia is a decentralized cloud storage platform that allows users to rent and share unused storage capacity. It offers secure, private, and cost-effective data storage solutions.

4. **Arweave**: Arweave is a permanent, decentralized archive for web-based content. It ensures that web content remains accessible and immutable over time.

4.2.5 Challenges and Future Directions

While decentralized file storage solutions offer numerous advantages, they also face challenges, including scalability, usability, and interoperability. The future of decentralized file storage will likely involve addressing these challenges, ensuring seamless integration with other Web 3.0 technologies.

Decentralized file storage is more than a technological shift; it's a shift in the power dynamics of the digital world. It empowers individuals to reclaim ownership of their data and engage with the internet in a more secure, private, and user-centric manner. As we navigate the decentralized internet's landscape, decentralized file storage is a critical pillar in the foundation of Web 3.0, reshaping the way we interact with and control our digital data.

4.3 Decentralized Domain Name Systems: Reimagining Internet Identity

The centralized nature of domain name systems (DNS) has long been a point of concern in the digital age. Centralized DNS providers have the power to control and manipulate domain names, which raises issues of censorship, security, and trust. In the Web 3.0 era, decentralized domain name systems are emerging as a transformative solution, putting the control of internet identity back into the hands of users.

4.3.1 Redefining Internet Identity

Decentralized domain name systems are a vital component of the Web 3.0 landscape. They offer an alternative to traditional DNS by leveraging blockchain and distributed ledger technologies to manage and allocate domain names. This shift to decentralization not only enhances the security and integrity of domain names but also promotes censorship resistance and user empowerment.

4.3.2 Key Elements of Decentralized Domain Name Systems

1. **Blockchain Integration**: Many decentralized domain name systems are built on blockchain technology, ensuring the transparency and security of domain name registrations.

2. **Decentralized Governance**: These systems often use decentralized governance models, allowing users to participate in the decision-making processes for domain allocation and management.

3. **Censorship Resistance**: Decentralized DNS systems make it difficult for authorities or entities to censor or control domain names, promoting a more open and inclusive internet.

4.3.3 Advantages of Decentralized Domain Name Systems

- **User Control**: Users have full control over their domain names, enabling them to manage their online identity without reliance on centralized authorities.

- **Censorship Resistance**: Decentralized domain names are resistant to censorship, ensuring that websites remain accessible even in regions with strict online controls.

- **Transparency**: Blockchain-based systems provide transparent and auditable domain name registrations, reducing the risk of fraudulent activities.

4.3.4 Real-World Applications

1. **Ethereum Name Service (ENS)**: ENS is a decentralized domain name system built on the Ethereum blockchain. It allows users to register and manage domain names ending in .eth. ENS has introduced a novel approach to internet identity and domain management.

2. **Handshake**: Handshake is a decentralized, peer-to-peer naming protocol that enables the creation and management of top-level domain names. It uses a blockchain-based naming system to ensure security and decentralization.

3. **Unstoppable Domains**: Unstoppable Domains offers domain names registered on the blockchain. These domain names are associated with cryptocurrency addresses, making them suitable for wallet addresses and decentralized applications.

4.3.5 Challenges and Future Directions

Decentralized domain name systems face challenges related to user adoption, interoperability with traditional DNS, and scalability. As they continue to evolve, these systems will need to address these challenges to gain broader acceptance and integration into the mainstream internet.

Decentralized domain name systems represent a significant step toward reclaiming internet identity and control. They empower users to own and manage their domain names securely and transparently, ensuring a more open and censorship-resistant online environment. As we navigate the evolving landscape of the decentralized internet, these systems are a cornerstone of the Web 3.0 vision, reshaping the way we interact with the digital world.

4.4 Building a Decentralized Internet: Navigating Web 3.0's Vision

The vision of a decentralized internet, often referred to as Web 3.0, is not a mere theoretical concept; it is a tangible and transformative endeavor that is reshaping the digital landscape. This vision centers on redefining the fundamental structure and principles of the internet, aiming to create a more equitable, secure, and user-centric online environment. Building a decentralized internet represents a profound shift in the way we access information, conduct transactions, and interact with the digital world.

4.4.1 The Foundation of a Decentralized Internet

At the heart of Web 3.0 is the aspiration to challenge the centralized nature of the current internet, which is characterized by the dominance of tech giants, data monopolies, and intermediaries. This vision hinges on the following foundational elements:

1. **Blockchain Technology**: Blockchain is the cornerstone of a decentralized internet. It ensures the immutability, transparency, and security of data. Blockchain underpins various Web 3.0 technologies and applications.

2. **Decentralized Applications (DApps)**: DApps operate on blockchain networks, eliminating the need for centralized servers. These applications offer services while keeping user data and transactions under their control.

3. **Smart Contracts**: Smart contracts automate and enforce agreements without intermediaries, enabling trustless transactions and introducing innovative use cases beyond finance.

4. **Peer-to-Peer (P2P) Networks**: P2P networks facilitate direct communication and data sharing between users, reducing reliance on centralized servers.

4.4.2 The Advantages of a Decentralized Internet

- **Data Ownership**: Users retain ownership and control of their data, deciding who can access and use it.

- **Privacy**: Decentralization enhances data privacy by reducing the risk of data breaches and unauthorized access.

- **Security**: Blockchain's encryption and immutability enhance data security, reducing the risk of data manipulation or loss.

- **Censorship Resistance**: A decentralized internet is resistant to censorship, ensuring open access to information.

4.4.3 Real-World Applications of Web 3.0

1. **Decentralized Finance (DeFi)**: DeFi platforms offer financial services without intermediaries, enabling users to lend, borrow, and trade assets directly on blockchain networks.

2. **Decentralized Identity**: Web 3.0 introduces decentralized identity solutions, allowing users to control and manage their online identity securely.

3. **Decentralized Applications (DApps)**: DApps span various domains, including finance, gaming, content creation, and more, offering innovative and user-centric experiences.

4.4.4 Challenges and Future Directions

While the vision of a decentralized internet holds immense promise, it is not without challenges. Scalability, regulatory compliance, usability, and interoperability are areas that need further development and attention. Web 3.0's evolution will involve addressing these challenges, ensuring its seamless integration into the broader digital landscape.

Web 3.0 is more than an abstract concept; it is a tangible movement that invites us to reimagine the internet as a decentralized, transparent, and user-focused ecosystem. As we navigate the ever-expanding frontiers of the decentralized internet, we are shaping a new digital landscape that empowers individuals, fosters trust, and redefines how we engage with the online world. Welcome to the era of Web 3.0 and the decentralized internet, where the vision of a more equitable, open, and user-empowered digital future becomes a reality.

4.5 Future Possibilities: Pioneering the Uncharted Territories of Web 3.0

Web 3.0, the decentralized internet, is not just a momentary disruption in the digital world; it's a transformative force that is continuously evolving, opening the door to an array of exciting possibilities and unprecedented opportunities. As we navigate the Web 3.0 landscape, we find ourselves on the threshold of a digital renaissance, where innovation knows no bounds, and the future is brimming with promise.

- **Decentralized Autonomous Organizations (DAOs):** Decentralized Autonomous Organizations are on the verge of redefining traditional corporate structures. DAOs are self-governing entities run by code and consensus, allowing participants to have a direct say in decision-making. They have the potential to revolutionize governance, enabling more transparent, efficient, and inclusive organizational structures.

- **Decentralized Identity and Self-Sovereign Identity:** In the decentralized internet, individuals have the opportunity to take control of their digital identities. Self-sovereign identity solutions provide users with a secure and portable way to manage their online persona, reducing reliance on centralized authorities and enhancing privacy.

- **Decentralized Finance (DeFi) Evolution:** DeFi is already transforming the financial sector, but its potential is far from exhausted. As DeFi matures, it may offer more complex financial instruments, increased liquidity, and further integration with traditional financial systems, providing financial services to the underserved and unbanked.

- **Digital Collectibles and Ownership:** The rise of non-fungible tokens (NFTs) and blockchain technology has sparked a revolution in digital ownership. The future holds possibilities for more diverse and interactive digital collectibles, as well as innovative methods of proving ownership for physical assets.

- **Enhanced Data Privacy and Security:** As Web 3.0 matures, we can expect more robust data privacy solutions. Advanced encryption techniques, zero-knowledge proofs, and decentralized storage will enhance data security, reducing the risks associated with centralized data breaches.

- **Interoperability and Cross-Chain Solutions:** The future of Web 3.0 will see a stronger emphasis on interoperability between various blockchain networks. Cross-chain solutions will enable seamless data and asset transfer across different platforms, fostering a more connected and efficient decentralized ecosystem.

- **Decentralized Governance Models:** Decentralized decision-making models, such as decentralized autonomous organizations (DAOs), will extend beyond finance and business to influence governance structures in the real world. These models may reshape political processes and introduce more transparent and participatory forms of governance.

- **Expanding DApp Ecosystem:** The DApp ecosystem will continue to expand, offering innovative solutions for industries ranging from healthcare and education to art and entertainment. The potential for creating user-centric, secure, and trustless applications is virtually limitless.

- **Web 3.0 in the Internet of Things (IoT):** As IoT devices become increasingly integrated into our lives, Web 3.0 could provide secure, decentralized infrastructure for managing and controlling these devices, ensuring data privacy and security.

- **Decentralized Internet Service Providers (ISPs):** The concept of decentralized ISPs is emerging, allowing users to participate in providing internet connectivity while removing the centralized control held by traditional ISPs.

Web 3.0 is not just a vision; it's an ongoing journey into a digital future that offers limitless potential. As we embrace the decentralized internet and navigate the Web 3.0 landscape, we become pioneers in a digital frontier that continues to evolve, innovate, and surprise. The possibilities are boundless, and the decentralized internet invites us to explore and shape the future of the digital world. Welcome to the era of Web 3.0, where we are not just observers but active participants in the reimagining of the internet.

Chapter 5: Blockchain-Based Identity and Privacy

In the evolving landscape of Web 3.0 and decentralized technologies, the way we establish and manage our digital identities is undergoing a profound transformation. This chapter delves into the critical intersection of blockchain technology, identity management, and privacy, offering insights into the innovative solutions that are reshaping how we navigate the digital realm.

5.1 The Challenge of Digital Identity

In the realm of Web 3.0 and decentralized technologies, one of the central challenges we encounter is redefining the concept of digital identity. The digital identity landscape of the previous era was characterized by its fragmented, centralized, and often insecure nature. Users were compelled to create and manage multiple identities across various online platforms, surrendering significant amounts of personal data to centralized authorities, leading to concerns regarding privacy and security. The challenge of digital identity in the Web 3.0 era is to transcend these limitations, enabling individuals to regain control over their online personas and transactions.

5.1.1 Fragmentation and Overexposure

The traditional digital identity landscape suffered from a fragmentation of identities across different websites and services. Users were required to create and manage multiple sets of credentials, each tied to a particular online platform. This fragmentation not only created inconvenience but also led to overexposure of personal data. Each time a user created a new identity online, they were essentially giving away a piece of themselves, risking their privacy.

5.1.2 Security and Trust Concerns

Centralized identity systems, operated by tech giants and service providers, held the keys to users' digital personas. This concentration of power resulted in security vulnerabilities and trust issues. High-profile data breaches and misuse of personal information underscored the urgent need for more secure, transparent, and user-centric identity solutions.

5.1.3 Empowering Self-Sovereign Identity

Web 3.0 seeks to address these challenges by introducing the concept of self-sovereign identity. Users are encouraged to take control of their own digital identities, deciding who has access to what parts of their personal information and transactions. Blockchain technology, with its security, transparency, and decentralized nature, plays a pivotal role in enabling self-sovereign identity.

5.1.4 Blockchain-Based Identity Solutions

Blockchain technology provides a foundation for secure and verifiable digital identity. It ensures that identity data is tamper-proof and transparent, reducing the risk of identity theft and fraud. Users can manage their identity credentials in a secure, decentralized manner, eliminating the need for third-party identity providers.

5.1.5 Challenges to Overcome

While blockchain-based identity solutions offer promise, challenges persist. Issues of scalability, usability, and integration with existing systems need to be addressed. Ensuring that the benefits of self-sovereign identity are accessible and practical for all users is a central concern.

The challenge of digital identity in the Web 3.0 era is an invitation to reimagine the way we establish and manage our online personas. It encourages us to move from fragmented, centralized identities to a more secure, user-centric, and privacy-respecting model. As we navigate the complexities of this challenge, we uncover opportunities to reshape the digital world, empowering individuals to take control of their digital lives and fostering a more open, secure, and user-friendly digital landscape.

5.2 Self-Sovereign Identity: Taking Control of Your Digital Persona

In the chapter on blockchain-based identity and privacy, one of the transformative concepts we explore is that of self-sovereign identity. Self-sovereign identity represents a fundamental shift in how individuals perceive and manage their digital personas in the Web 3.0 era. It empowers users to assert control over their online identities, reducing their reliance on centralized authorities and enabling secure, user-centric digital interactions.

5.2.1 Defining Self-Sovereign Identity

Self-sovereign identity, often abbreviated as SSI, is a user-centric approach to identity management. It gives individuals the ability to own, control, and share their identity data according to their preferences, without the need for intermediaries. This concept aligns perfectly with the principles of decentralization, blockchain technology, and user empowerment.

5.2.2 Key Characteristics of Self-Sovereign Identity

1. **User Control**: SSI grants individuals complete control over their identity data, determining who can access and use it. Users can decide what information to disclose for each specific interaction.

2. **Decentralization**: Self-sovereign identity systems often rely on decentralized blockchain networks to ensure the security, integrity, and tamper resistance of identity data.

3. **Privacy**: SSI enhances data privacy by minimizing the exposure of personal information. Users only share necessary details for specific transactions or interactions.

5.2.3 The Role of Blockchain in Self-Sovereign Identity

Blockchain technology plays a pivotal role in enabling self-sovereign identity. It provides a tamper-proof ledger that ensures the integrity of identity data, reducing the risk of data breaches, identity theft, and fraud. The transparency and security of blockchain align perfectly with the principles of SSI, fostering trust between parties in digital interactions.

5.2.4 Use Cases of Self-Sovereign Identity

1. **Secure Login and Authentication**: Users can access services and platforms securely without the need to

remember multiple passwords. SSI ensures that only necessary information is shared for authentication.

2. **Online Identity Verification**: SSI offers a more secure and privacy-respecting way to verify one's identity for various online services, from financial transactions to social interactions.

3. **Reducing Data Exposure**: With SSI, users can interact with services and platforms without revealing more personal information than necessary, minimizing their digital footprint.

5.2.5 Challenges and the Road Ahead

While self-sovereign identity holds immense promise, challenges persist, including user adoption, interoperability, and regulatory considerations. Ensuring that SSI is accessible and practical for all users is a central concern.

Self-sovereign identity marks a profound shift in how we manage our digital personas. It empowers individuals to take control of their online identities, fostering a more secure, user-centric, and privacy-respecting digital environment. As we explore the possibilities of self-sovereign identity in the context of blockchain-based identity and privacy, we uncover the potential to reshape the way we interact with the digital world, one where individuals truly own their digital selves.

5.3 Privacy and Data Ownership: Web 3.0's Cornerstones

In the chapter on blockchain-based identity and privacy, we dive deep into two fundamental principles that are reshaping the digital landscape in the Web 3.0 era: privacy and data ownership. These principles address the concerns that have long plagued the centralized internet—concerns about data security, user privacy, and control over personal information.

5.3.1 Privacy in the Digital Age

The digital age brought unprecedented opportunities for communication, innovation, and connectivity. However, it also gave rise to a growing concern: the erosion of privacy. Centralized internet platforms often require users to share extensive personal data, which they monetize for targeted advertising and other purposes. This has resulted in an environment where users' online behaviors are closely monitored, raising significant privacy concerns.

5.3.2 Web 3.0's Privacy Revolution

Web 3.0 challenges this status quo by putting user privacy at the forefront. Blockchain-based identity and privacy solutions allow users to interact online while revealing only the information necessary for each specific transaction or interaction. This approach minimizes the exposure of personal data, reducing the risk of data breaches and identity theft.

5.3.3 Data Ownership: A New Paradigm

In the Web 3.0 era, data ownership is transferred from centralized entities to individuals. Blockchain technology, with its transparency, immutability, and security, underpins this shift. Users own their data and have the final say on how it is used. They can choose to monetize their data or keep it entirely private.

5.3.4 Key Concepts to Explore

1. **Selective Data Disclosure**: Web 3.0 enables users to practice selective data disclosure. When interacting with services or platforms, users can decide what information to share and what to keep private.

2. **Privacy-Enhancing Technologies (PETs)**: PETs such as zero-knowledge proofs and advanced encryption methods are central to maintaining privacy in decentralized interactions.

3. **Data Monetization**: Web 3.0 introduces the possibility of users benefiting from their data. They can choose to share data for compensation, reversing the data monetization paradigm.

5.3.5 Use Cases of Privacy and Data Ownership

1. **Secure Transactions**: In financial transactions, users can securely share necessary financial details without exposing their entire financial history.

2. **Healthcare**: Patients can share only specific health records with healthcare providers, enhancing privacy and security.

3. **Online Shopping**: Users can shop online without revealing their entire purchasing history or personal information.

5.3.6 Challenges and Future Directions

While the principles of privacy and data ownership are central to Web 3.0, challenges remain. These include ensuring user adoption, addressing regulatory considerations, and enhancing user education on privacy-enhancing tools and techniques.

The chapter on blockchain-based identity and privacy encourages us to reflect on the transformation of our digital lives. It brings us into a world where privacy is respected, data ownership is reclaimed, and individuals regain control over their digital personas. As we navigate this landscape, we discover new possibilities for a more secure, user-centric, and privacy-respecting digital future.

5.4 Decentralized Identity Platforms: The Key to Secure, User-Centric Identity

In the chapter on blockchain-based identity and privacy, we explore how decentralized identity platforms are revolutionizing the way individuals establish and manage their digital personas in the Web 3.0 era. These platforms are at the forefront of a transformative movement, providing secure, user-centric, and privacy-respecting solutions that transcend the limitations of the centralized internet.

5.4.1 The Centralized Identity Quandary

Centralized identity systems have long been the standard on the internet. Users are required to create numerous accounts across various platforms, each one demanding a distinct set of credentials. The overexposure of personal data and the risk of data breaches have been persistent concerns in this model. Users often have little control over their own identity information.

5.4.2 Decentralized Identity: A Paradigm Shift

Decentralized identity platforms represent a paradigm shift in the Web 3.0 era. They place individuals at the center of identity management, enabling users to assert control over their digital identities, share data only as necessary, and reduce reliance on third-party identity providers.

5.4.3 Key Features of Decentralized Identity Platforms

1. **User-Centricity**: Decentralized identity platforms prioritize the interests of the user, giving them control over their identity data.

2. **Interoperability**: These platforms are designed to be interoperable, allowing users to manage their identities across various services and applications seamlessly.

3. **Security**: The use of blockchain technology ensures the security and integrity of identity data, reducing the risk of identity theft and data breaches.

5.4.4 The Role of Blockchain in Decentralized Identity

Blockchain technology is integral to the functioning of decentralized identity platforms. It provides the necessary features of transparency, immutability, and security. Users' identity data is stored on a decentralized ledger, ensuring that it remains tamper-proof and resistant to unauthorized alterations.

5.4.5 Use Cases of Decentralized Identity Platforms

1. **Secure Login and Authentication**: Users can access services and platforms securely without having to remember multiple passwords. Instead, they use their decentralized identity credentials.

2. **Online Identity Verification**: For various online services, from financial transactions to social media interactions, decentralized identity platforms offer a secure and privacy-respecting method of verifying one's identity.

3. **Reduced Data Exposure**: Users can interact with services and platforms without revealing more personal information than necessary, minimizing their digital footprint.

5.4.6 Challenges and the Road Ahead

While decentralized identity platforms hold immense potential, challenges remain, including user adoption, integration with existing systems, and regulatory considerations. Ensuring that these platforms are accessible and practical for all users is a central concern.

The chapter on blockchain-based identity and privacy invites us to explore the transformative potential of decentralized identity platforms. It allows us to envision a digital future where individuals truly own and control their digital identities, where data exposure is minimized, and where privacy and security are paramount. In this new era, individuals are not just users but active participants in the reimagining of digital identity.

5.5 Identity and Web 3.0: A Paradigm Shift in Blockchain-Based Identity and Privacy

In the chapter on blockchain-based identity and privacy, we embark on a journey to understand the profound implications of identity in the Web 3.0 era. This transformative chapter underscores the pivotal role of blockchain technology in reshaping how individuals establish and safeguard their digital identities, fostering a more secure, user-centric, and privacy-respecting internet.

5.5.1 Identity in the Digital Age

In the digital age, our identities are no longer confined to the physical realm. Online, we assume digital personas, each linked to our activities, transactions, and interactions. Traditional identity systems have long been characterized by fragmentation, centralization, and a lack of user control.

5.5.2 Web 3.0: Redefining Digital Identity

Web 3.0 challenges this status quo by placing digital identity under the spotlight. This new era is defined by decentralization, user empowerment, and a reimagining of digital identity. Blockchain technology emerges as a powerful enabler of this shift, offering security, transparency, and user control.

5.5.3 Key Themes in Identity and Web 3.0

1. **User Control**: Web 3.0 emphasizes user control over digital identities. Individuals can determine what information to disclose and to whom, creating a more private and secure online environment.

2. **Decentralization**: Blockchain technology, with its decentralized ledger, ensures the security and transparency of identity data, minimizing the risk of data breaches and identity theft.

3. **Privacy**: Web 3.0 prioritizes privacy by enabling users to share only necessary identity information for specific interactions, reducing the digital footprint.

5.5.4 The Role of Blockchain in Identity

Blockchain technology provides the backbone for reimagining digital identity. It acts as a tamper-proof, transparent ledger where identity data is stored. This ensures data integrity and security, fostering trust in online interactions.

5.5.5 Use Cases in Identity and Web 3.0

1. **Secure Digital Transactions**: Blockchain-based identity solutions facilitate secure transactions, allowing users to access services without extensive exposure of personal information.

2. **Online Verification**: Users can securely verify their identity online for various services, including financial transactions, with a focus on security and privacy.

3. **Selective Data Sharing**: Web 3.0 encourages selective data sharing, meaning users can interact with services without divulging more information than necessary.

5.5.6 Challenges and Future Directions

As we navigate the path toward redefined digital identity in Web 3.0, we encounter challenges such as user adoption, integration with existing systems, and regulatory considerations. Ensuring that these innovations are practical and accessible for all users remains a central concern.

The chapter on blockchain-based identity and privacy invites us to envision a digital future where individuals truly own and control their online personas, reducing data exposure, enhancing privacy, and prioritizing security. In this era, individuals are not just passive users but active participants in the evolution of digital identity.

Chapter 6: Web 3.0 and Finance

In the chapter on "Web 3.0 and Finance" within our exploration of decentralized technologies, we embark on a journey that reveals the profound transformation underway in the world of finance. The arrival of Web 3.0, marked by decentralization, blockchain technology, and user empowerment, has set in motion a paradigm shift that challenges the conventions of the traditional financial industry.

The financial landscape of Web 3.0 is a departure from the centralized, intermediated systems that have dominated the financial sector for centuries. Centralized authorities, legacy banking institutions, and a lack of transparency have, at times, left individuals disempowered and excluded from the global financial conversation.

6.1 Decentralized Finance (DeFi): Transforming the Financial World in Web 3.0

In the chapter on "Web 3.0 and Finance," we explore one of the most exciting and transformative innovations of our time: Decentralized Finance, or DeFi. DeFi represents a seismic shift in the way we think about and interact with the world of finance, and it is at the forefront of the Web 3.0 revolution.

6.1.1 The Traditional Financial System

Traditional finance, characterized by banks, intermediaries, and centralized control, has long been the standard. However, this system has been plagued by limitations, including high transaction costs, limited accessibility, and a lack of transparency.

6.1.2 DeFi's Core Principles

DeFi is rooted in the principles of Web 3.0, emphasizing decentralization, transparency, and inclusivity. It leverages blockchain technology, particularly smart contracts, to create a borderless and permissionless financial ecosystem.

6.1.3 Key Features of DeFi

1. **Peer-to-Peer Transactions**: DeFi eliminates the need for intermediaries, allowing individuals to engage in direct peer-to-peer financial interactions.

2. **Interoperability**: DeFi protocols are designed to be interoperable, enabling users to access a wide range of financial services within a single, interconnected ecosystem.

3. **Transparency**: The use of blockchain ensures complete transparency of transactions, reducing the risk of fraud and manipulation.

6.1.4 DeFi Use Cases

1. **Lending and Borrowing**: DeFi platforms enable individuals to lend their assets and earn interest or borrow assets without the need for a traditional bank.

2. **Decentralized Exchanges (DEXs)**: These platforms allow users to trade cryptocurrencies without relying on centralized exchanges.

3. **Stablecoins**: DeFi introduces stablecoins, which are cryptocurrencies pegged to real-world assets like the US dollar, providing stability in a volatile market.

4. **Yield Farming and Liquidity Provision**: Users can earn rewards by providing liquidity to DeFi platforms.

6.1.5 Challenges and Opportunities

While DeFi offers immense potential, it also presents challenges such as regulatory compliance, security vulnerabilities, and the need for user education. Additionally, the fast-paced nature of DeFi development requires users to stay informed about the latest advancements.

The chapter on "Web 3.0 and Finance" delves into DeFi as a groundbreaking force, one that has the potential to democratize finance, increase financial inclusion, and provide innovative financial services to individuals worldwide. As we navigate this financial frontier, we gain insight into a decentralized, user-centric, and globally accessible financial future.

6.2 Cryptocurrencies and Digital Assets: The New Currency of Web 3.0 Finance

In the chapter on "Web 3.0 and Finance," we venture into the realm of cryptocurrencies and digital assets, where cutting-edge technologies and decentralized principles converge to reshape the financial landscape. This transformative financial frontier, rooted in Web 3.0 principles, challenges traditional currency and asset models, offering a new way to transact, invest, and store value.

6.2.1 The Rise of Digital Assets

The emergence of digital assets, often in the form of cryptocurrencies, marks a departure from traditional fiat currencies and physical assets. These digital entities exist on blockchain networks, bringing transparency, security, and user empowerment to the world of finance.

6.2.2 Key Concepts in Cryptocurrencies and Digital Assets

1. **Decentralization**: Cryptocurrencies are decentralized and operate on distributed ledger technology. This decentralization eliminates the need for intermediaries, like banks, in financial transactions.

2. **Blockchain Technology**: Blockchain underpins digital assets, ensuring transparency, immutability, and security. Transactions are recorded on a public ledger, making them verifiable and tamper-resistant.

3. **Security**: Cryptocurrencies offer enhanced security, reducing the risk of fraud, identity theft, and unauthorized access to financial assets.

6.2.3 Use Cases of Cryptocurrencies and Digital Assets

1. **Digital Cash**: Cryptocurrencies like Bitcoin and Litecoin offer a secure and efficient way to conduct peer-to-peer transactions without the need for physical cash.

2. **Investments**: Many investors view digital assets as a new asset class, diversifying their portfolios with cryptocurrencies such as Ethereum and digital tokens representing real-world assets.

3. **Smart Contracts**: Cryptocurrencies enable the execution of self-executing smart contracts, automating agreements without intermediaries.

6.2.4 Challenges and Opportunities

The adoption and mainstream acceptance of cryptocurrencies and digital assets bring both opportunities and challenges. Regulatory scrutiny, security concerns, and the need for user education are among the key considerations. Additionally, the volatility of digital asset prices underscores the need for a thorough understanding of this evolving market.

The chapter on "Web 3.0 and Finance" introduces us to the transformative potential of cryptocurrencies and digital assets. In this chapter, we explore how these innovations are reshaping the financial industry, fostering a more inclusive, secure, and user-centric financial ecosystem. As we navigate this dynamic landscape, we gain insight into the evolving nature of money and asset ownership in the digital age.

6.3 Automated Finance (Afi): The Future of Financial Management in Web 3.0

In the chapter on "Web 3.0 and Finance," we delve into the innovative realm of Automated Finance, often abbreviated as Afi. Afi represents a groundbreaking development at the intersection of finance, blockchain technology, and automation, offering a glimpse into the future of financial management in the Web 3.0 era.

6.3.1 Redefining Financial Management

Automated Finance, or Afi, is transforming how individuals manage their finances. It leverages blockchain technology and smart contracts to automate a wide range of financial processes, from investing to savings and even risk management.

6.3.2 Key Concepts in Automated Finance (Afi)

1. **Smart Contracts**: Afi relies on smart contracts, self-executing agreements that automatically enforce the terms of a financial arrangement. This automation reduces the need for intermediaries.

2. **Decentralization**: Afi systems operate on decentralized platforms, ensuring security, transparency, and user empowerment.

3. **Algorithmic Decision-Making**: Afi often involves algorithmic decision-making, which utilizes data and predefined rules to make financial decisions.

6.3.3 Use Cases of Automated Finance (Afi)

1. **Automated Investment Portfolios**: Afi systems create and manage investment portfolios based on user-defined goals and risk tolerance.

2. **Decentralized Lending and Borrowing**: Afi platforms enable users to lend or borrow assets without the need for traditional banks.

3. **Automated Risk Management**: Afi systems monitor financial risks and automatically adjust investment strategies to mitigate losses.

6.3.4 Challenges and Opportunities

Afi presents a new frontier in financial management, promising efficiency, reduced costs, and democratization of financial services. However, it also brings challenges, including the need for regulatory frameworks and addressing potential algorithmic biases.

The chapter on "Web 3.0 and Finance" invites us to explore Automated Finance (Afi) as a revolutionary force in reshaping how individuals manage their finances. As we navigate this financial frontier, we gain insight into a more automated, accessible, and user-centric approach to financial management, enabled by Web 3.0 principles and blockchain technology.

6.4 Challenges and Regulatory Concerns: Navigating the Web 3.0 Finance Landscape

In this chapter we delve into the transformative potential of decentralized technologies, cryptocurrencies, and automated financial systems. However, this financial frontier is not without its share of challenges and regulatory concerns. As we navigate the evolving landscape of Web 3.0 finance, we encounter a range of issues that must be addressed for the long-term sustainability and security of the digital financial ecosystem.

6.4.1 Key Challenges in Web 3.0 Finance

1. **Regulatory Uncertainty**: One of the primary challenges in Web 3.0 finance is the lack of a consistent and comprehensive regulatory framework. Different countries and regions have adopted varied approaches to regulating cryptocurrencies and decentralized financial services, leading to uncertainty for users and service providers.

2. **Security Vulnerabilities**: While blockchain technology is known for its security features, it is not immune to vulnerabilities. Hacks, fraud, and vulnerabilities in smart contracts have led to substantial financial losses, necessitating a continuous focus on improving security measures.

3. **User Education**: Web 3.0 finance introduces complex concepts and technologies. Many users lack the knowledge and understanding necessary to navigate this new landscape safely. User education is critical to ensuring that individuals can protect their assets and make informed financial decisions.

4. **Market Volatility**: The cryptocurrency market is known for its price volatility. While this volatility can

present opportunities for investors, it also poses risks, including substantial financial losses.

6.4.2 Regulatory Concerns

1. **Consumer Protection**: Regulators are concerned about ensuring the protection of consumers in Web 3.0 finance, particularly regarding fraud, scams, and misleading financial products.

2. **Anti-Money Laundering (AML) and Know Your Customer (KYC) Regulations**: Regulators are keen on preventing illicit activities, and AML and KYC regulations aim to address these concerns. However, striking a balance between privacy and compliance remains a challenge.

3. **Taxation**: The tax implications of cryptocurrency transactions and decentralized finance activities vary from one jurisdiction to another. Clarity on tax obligations is necessary.

4. **Market Integrity**: Regulators seek to ensure the integrity of financial markets in the face of potential market manipulation and fraud.

6.4.3 Opportunities for Regulatory Innovation

The regulatory landscape for Web 3.0 finance is still evolving. Regulators have the opportunity to adapt to these new technologies and develop innovative regulatory frameworks that balance the need for user protection with the promotion of innovation and financial inclusion.

As we navigate the complexities of Web 3.0 finance, addressing these challenges and regulatory concerns becomes crucial for the long-term success and security of the digital financial ecosystem. It is a dynamic space where industry participants, regulators, and users must collaborate to shape a financial future that benefits all.

6.5 The Future of Financial Services: Web 3.0 and Beyond

In this section we cast our gaze into the future, exploring the transformative potential of Web 3.0 technologies in redefining the landscape of financial services. This futuristic vision transcends traditional boundaries, presenting a financial ecosystem that is more inclusive, accessible, and empowered by decentralization.

6.5.1 Web 3.0 Principles Shaping the Future

The future of financial services is inexorably tied to the principles of Web 3.0, including decentralization, transparency, and user empowerment.

1. Decentralization: Decentralization is a foundational principle of Web 3.0 finance. It eliminates the need for traditional intermediaries, putting control directly into the hands of individuals. This shift empowers users to transact, invest, and manage their financial assets without relying on centralized authorities.

2. Transparency: Blockchain technology ensures transparency in financial transactions. Every transaction is recorded on a public ledger, allowing users to verify and trust the integrity of the financial system.

3. Accessibility: Web 3.0 finance aims to broaden financial inclusion, ensuring that individuals worldwide, including those who are unbanked or underbanked, can participate in the global economy.

6.5.2 Future Trends in Financial Services

1. **Decentralized Banking**: Traditional banks may face competition from decentralized financial institutions. These institutions offer a range of services, including lending, borrowing, and earning interest, all through decentralized platforms.

2. **Tokenized Assets**: The future may see a proliferation of tokenized assets, allowing for the fractional ownership of real-world assets like real estate, art, and more. This democratizes investment opportunities.

3. **Personal Financial Assistants**: AI-driven personal financial assistants may become common, helping users manage their assets, make informed financial decisions, and automate routine financial tasks.

4. **Automated Risk Management**: Afi (Automated Finance) systems will offer advanced risk management solutions, automatically adjusting investment strategies to mitigate potential losses.

6.5.3 Challenges and Opportunities

The future of financial services in Web 3.0 is not without its challenges. Regulatory adaptation, user education, and security enhancements are essential to ensure the success of these transformative technologies.

This section invites us to envision a future where financial services are more inclusive, transparent, and directly under the control of individuals. As we navigate this landscape, we prepare ourselves for a financial future that transcends borders, reduces barriers to entry, and fosters a more equitable and user-centric global financial ecosystem.

Chapter 7: Web 3.0 and the Evolution of Supply Chain Management

In the chapter dedicated to "Web 3.0 and the Evolution of Supply Chain Management," we embark on a journey through the transformative power of Web 3.0 technologies in redefining the world of supply chain management. The advent of blockchain, the Internet of Things (IoT), and decentralized technologies is ushering in a new era of transparency, efficiency, and sustainability in the global supply chain.

The Traditional Supply Chain

Traditional supply chain management has long been characterized by a lack of transparency, complexity, and inefficiency. In this model, goods and information flow through a web of intermediaries, often obscuring the origins and journey of products from manufacturer to consumer.

The Promise of Web 3.0 in Supply Chain

Web 3.0 technologies are poised to address these long-standing challenges, ushering in a more transparent and streamlined supply chain.

7.1 Traceability and Transparency: Revolutionizing Supply Chain Management in Web 3.0

In this section we explore the groundbreaking concepts of traceability and transparency that are reshaping the global supply chain landscape. Web 3.0 technologies, such as blockchain and the Internet of Things (IoT), are unlocking new dimensions of trust and accountability, fostering a more responsible and efficient supply chain.

7.1.1 The Challenge of Traceability

Traditional supply chains have often struggled with traceability. The journey of products from origin to consumer has been shrouded in opacity, making it difficult to verify the authenticity, quality, and ethical sourcing of goods. This lack of transparency has led to issues like counterfeit products, unsafe supply chains, and unsustainable practices.

7.1.2 The Promise of Web 3.0 in Traceability

Web 3.0 technologies offer a robust solution to the traceability challenge. Through blockchain and IoT integration, they enable the creation of transparent, immutable, and fully traceable supply chains.

7.1.3 Blockchain's Role in Traceability

1. **Immutable Records**: Blockchain's distributed ledger technology ensures that records are tamper-proof, providing an unbroken chain of custody for each product.
2. **Provenance Tracking**: Blockchain allows every participant in the supply chain, from manufacturers to distributors and consumers, to trace the journey of products with full confidence in the accuracy of the data.

7.1.4 The Internet of Things (IoT) in Traceability

1. **Real-time Monitoring**: IoT devices and sensors attached to products provide real-time data on their location, temperature, humidity, and more. This data ensures that goods are kept under optimal conditions throughout their journey.

2. **Automated Data Collection**: IoT automates data collection, reducing human error and enhancing the accuracy of tracking and traceability.

7.1.5 Use Cases of Traceability and Transparency in Web 3.0 Supply Chain

1. **Food Safety**: Consumers can verify the safety and origin of food products, reducing the risk of foodborne illnesses.

2. **Ethical Sourcing**: Traceability enables consumers to support businesses that adhere to ethical sourcing practices.

3. **Counterfeit Prevention**: Luxury brands and manufacturers can protect their intellectual property and consumers from counterfeit products.

7.1.6 Challenges and Opportunities

While Web 3.0 technologies promise unparalleled traceability and transparency, they also bring challenges, including data privacy, standardization, and integration across supply chain participants. Overcoming these challenges is essential for the continued success of a more transparent and accountable supply chain.

This section encourages us to envision a future where products' journey from origin to consumption is fully traceable and transparent. As we explore this transformative landscape, we gain insight into how these technologies are enabling responsible sourcing, reducing fraud, and fostering a more ethical and sustainable supply chain ecosystem.

7.2 Blockchain in Supply Chain: Revolutionizing Transparency and Trust

In this section we dive deep into the transformative role of blockchain technology in redefining how supply chains operate. Blockchain is heralding an era of unprecedented transparency, traceability, and trust in the global supply chain, making it a cornerstone of Web 3.0 supply chain management.

7.2.1 Understanding Blockchain's Impact

1. **Immutable Ledger**: Blockchain technology is fundamentally a decentralized and immutable ledger. Every transaction recorded on a blockchain is permanent, tamper-proof, and transparent to all participants. This immutability ensures trust and security within the supply chain.

2. **Smart Contracts**: Smart contracts are self-executing agreements with the terms of the contract written directly into code. These contracts automatically execute actions when predefined conditions are met, reducing the need for intermediaries and minimizing the risk of errors or disputes.

7.2.2 Key Benefits of Blockchain in Supply Chain

1. **Enhanced Traceability**: Blockchain allows for the seamless tracking of products from their origin to the hands of consumers. Every stage of the supply chain is recorded, ensuring that the history and authenticity of products are verifiable.

2. **Reduced Fraud**: Counterfeit goods and fraudulent activities within the supply chain become nearly impossible due to the transparency and immutability of blockchain records.

3. **Streamlined Processes**: Smart contracts automate various processes, including payments, quality control, and inventory management, resulting in increased efficiency and reduced delays.

4. **Improved Trust**: Blockchain's transparency and security measures instill trust among supply chain participants, fostering stronger relationships and accountability.

7.2.3 Use Cases of Blockchain in Supply Chain

1. **Food Safety**: Consumers can trace the origin of food products, helping prevent foodborne illnesses and enabling companies to quickly address recalls.

2. **Pharmaceuticals**: Blockchain verifies the authenticity of medications, reducing the risk of counterfeit drugs entering the market.

3. **Ethical Sourcing**: Companies can ensure that their products are sourced ethically, promoting sustainability and responsible business practices.

7.2.4 Challenges and Adoption

While the potential benefits of blockchain in supply chain management are immense, challenges include integration, data privacy, and standardization. Companies need to navigate these challenges to fully adopt this transformative technology.

This section allows us to envision a future where supply chains are characterized by transparency, accountability, and security. Blockchain, as a foundational technology of Web 3.0, is reshaping how goods are produced, distributed, and consumed, forging a more trustworthy and efficient supply chain ecosystem.

7.3 Smart Contracts for Supply Chain: Streamlining Operations in Web 3.0

Within this section we explore the revolutionary role of smart contracts in reshaping the landscape of supply chain operations. Smart contracts, an integral component of blockchain technology, are enabling a new era of efficiency, automation, and trust in supply chain management.

7.3.1 Understanding Smart Contracts

Smart contracts are self-executing agreements with the terms of the contract directly encoded into code. These contracts automatically execute actions when predefined conditions are met. They operate on the "if-then" principle, ensuring that parties involved can trust the execution of contract terms without the need for intermediaries.

7.3.2 Key Features of Smart Contracts in Supply Chain

1. **Automation**: Smart contracts automate various supply chain processes, such as payments, quality control, and inventory management, reducing the need for manual intervention.

2. **Transparency**: The terms of smart contracts are stored on a blockchain, ensuring that all relevant parties can verify the terms and conditions of the agreement. This transparency fosters trust and accountability.

3. **Immutability**: Once a smart contract is deployed, its code and execution cannot be altered, making it tamper-proof and secure.

7.3.3 Benefits of Smart Contracts in Supply Chain

1. **Efficiency**: Automation reduces delays and errors in supply chain processes, leading to faster and more streamlined operations.

2. **Reduced Costs**: Smart contracts eliminate the need for intermediaries, lowering operational costs and increasing cost-effectiveness.

3. **Transparency and Trust**: Parties can trust in the execution of contract terms, knowing that the blockchain records provide a verifiable and unchangeable history of events.

7.3.4 Use Cases of Smart Contracts in Supply Chain

1. **Payment Automation**: Upon delivery of goods or services, smart contracts can automatically trigger payments, reducing delays in the settlement process.

2. **Quality Control**: IoT devices can provide real-time data on the quality of products. If products fail to meet predefined quality standards, smart contracts can initiate actions, such as returning or replacing the products.

3. **Inventory Management**: Smart contracts can manage inventory levels and automatically reorder supplies when stock is low, ensuring a consistent supply of goods.

7.3.5 Challenges and Implementation

The adoption of smart contracts in supply chain management requires overcoming challenges related to integration, ensuring the security of contract code, and educating supply chain participants on this transformative technology.

In this section we delve into the potential of smart contracts to enhance efficiency, accountability, and trust within the supply chain. As we explore this technological frontier, we envision a future where supply chains are characterized by automation and transparency, ushering in a new era of responsible and efficient global commerce.

7.4 Real-World Examples: Web 3.0's Impact on Supply Chain Management

In this section we take a closer look at real-world applications that demonstrate the transformative potential of Web 3.0 technologies in supply chain management. These examples showcase how blockchain, the Internet of Things (IoT), and smart contracts are already revolutionizing the global supply chain.

7.4.1 IBM Food Trust:

IBM Food Trust is a blockchain-based platform that focuses on ensuring the safety and transparency of the food supply chain. This system enables end-to-end traceability of food products, allowing consumers to verify the origin and authenticity of the food they purchase. The platform has been used to track a wide range of food items, from mangoes to beef, creating a more secure and accountable supply chain.

7.4.2 Provenance in the Tuna Industry

The tuna industry has been plagued by issues related to illegal fishing and sustainability. Provenance, a blockchain-based startup, has partnered with the tuna industry to create a transparent and sustainable supply chain for tuna. Consumers can scan a QR code on a tuna product to access information about its journey from the ocean to the store shelf, ensuring ethical sourcing and responsible fishing practices.

7.4.3 De Beers and Diamond Tracking

De Beers, a renowned diamond company, has turned to blockchain to trace the journey of diamonds from the mine to the consumer. This initiative, called Tracr, ensures that diamonds are sourced responsibly and ethically. It also prevents the entry of conflict or "blood" diamonds into the market by creating an immutable record of each diamond's history.

7.4.4 Maersk and TradeLens:

Maersk, one of the world's largest shipping companies, has partnered with IBM to create TradeLens, a blockchain platform for global trade. TradeLens digitizes the documentation and approval processes in shipping, reducing the time and costs involved in moving goods across international borders. This initiative streamlines the global supply chain and ensures the integrity of trade data.

7.4.5 Walmart and VeChain for Food Safety:

Retail giant Walmart, in collaboration with VeChain, has employed blockchain technology to enhance food safety. By leveraging VeChain's blockchain, Walmart tracks products like pork and leafy greens from farms to store shelves. In the event of a food recall, the supply chain can be quickly and accurately traced, reducing the impact on consumers.

These real-world examples illustrate how Web 3.0 technologies are already transforming supply chain management. They provide transparency, traceability, and efficiency, making supply chains more responsible, accountable, and secure. As we explore these applications in the chapter, we gain valuable insights into how these technologies are redefining the way we produce, distribute, and consume goods in the 21st century.

7.5 Challenges and Future Trends in Web 3.0 Supply Chain Management

As we journey through the chapter on "Web 3.0 and Supply Chain Management," it's imperative to recognize the challenges and future trends that shape this transformative landscape. The adoption of Web 3.0 technologies in supply chain management is a promising endeavor, but it comes with its set of hurdles and evolving trends.

7.5.1 Challenges

1. **Integration and Interoperability**: The integration of Web 3.0 technologies into existing supply chain

systems can be complex. Ensuring that different platforms and technologies work seamlessly together is a substantial challenge.

2. **Data Privacy and Security**: The transparent nature of blockchain can raise concerns about data privacy. Supply chain participants need to carefully manage and secure sensitive information while maintaining transparency.

3. **Standardization**: For Web 3.0 technologies to reach their full potential, industry-wide standards must be established. A lack of standardization can hinder adoption and interoperability.

4. **Education and Adoption**: Training supply chain participants to understand and embrace these technologies is crucial. A lack of education and familiarity can delay adoption and the realization of benefits.

5. **Regulatory Compliance**: Navigating the evolving regulatory landscape for Web 3.0 technologies, especially in global supply chains, presents challenges for companies and organizations.

7.5.2 Future Trends

1. **Wider Adoption**: As awareness and understanding of Web 3.0 technologies grow, a broader range of

industries and supply chain participants will adopt these solutions.

2. **IoT Integration**: The integration of IoT devices with blockchain for real-time tracking and monitoring of goods will become more prevalent. This will provide a higher level of transparency and accountability.

3. **Cross-Chain Platforms**: The development of interoperable cross-chain platforms will enable different blockchains to work together seamlessly, enhancing the efficiency of supply chain operations.

4. **AI and Machine Learning**: AI and machine learning will play an increasingly important role in supply chain decision-making, optimizing routes, demand forecasting, and quality control.

5. **Circular Economy**: Blockchain and smart contracts will enable the emergence of circular supply chains, where products are designed for reuse and recycling, promoting sustainability.

6. **Tokenization**: The use of blockchain tokens for assets, products, and even supply chain financing will offer new opportunities for stakeholders.

7. **Decentralized Autonomous Organizations (DAOs)**: The concept of DAOs may reshape supply chain governance and decision-making, enabling a more decentralized and autonomous approach.

8. **Quantum-Safe Blockchain**: As quantum computing advances, ensuring the security of blockchain networks will become critical. Quantum-safe blockchain technologies will be a future trend.

Understanding the challenges and anticipating future trends in Web 3.0 supply chain management is essential for organizations and individuals looking to harness the full potential of these technologies. The future promises a more efficient, transparent, and sustainable supply chain ecosystem, but it also calls for proactive measures to address challenges and keep pace with an ever-evolving digital landscape.

Chapter 8: Shaping the Future of Content Publishing in Web 3.0

In the chapter dedicated to "Web 3.0 and Content Publishing" we embark on a journey into the transformative world of content creation and dissemination in the era of Web 3.0. Web 3.0, with its decentralized technologies and innovative approaches, promises to redefine how content is produced, distributed, consumed, and even monetized.

The advent of the internet, often referred to as Web 1.0, brought static web pages and basic information sharing. Web 2.0 ushered in an era of dynamic user-generated content, social media, and interactivity. Now, we find ourselves on the cusp of Web 3.0, which holds the potential to bring about the next evolution in content publishing.

Web 3.0 is characterized by the integration of blockchain, decentralized applications (DApps), and various other cutting-edge technologies into the fabric of the internet. These technologies promise to not only address some of the limitations of the previous web iterations but also introduce novel concepts and paradigms that will reshape the digital content landscape.

8.1 Decentralized Content Platforms: A Paradigm Shift in Web 3.0 Content Publishing

In this section we delve into the dynamic realm of decentralized content platforms, a revolutionary concept that has the potential to transform the way content is created, shared, and monetized in the digital landscape.

8.1.1 The Emergence of Decentralized Content Platforms

Web 3.0 brings with it the promise of decentralized technologies, blockchain-based platforms, and decentralized applications (DApps) that challenge the status quo of content publishing. These platforms are designed to empower content creators, authors, artists, and influencers in unprecedented ways.

8.1.2 Key Features and Benefits

1. **Ownership and Control**: Decentralized content platforms enable creators to retain ownership and control over their content. Content is stored on decentralized networks, ensuring that creators have a say in how their work is used and shared.

2. **Copyright Protection**: Blockchain technology provides a transparent and immutable record of content ownership and usage. This not only protects creators from unauthorized usage but also simplifies the enforcement of copyright.

3. **Monetization Opportunities**: Web 3.0 content platforms offer diverse monetization options. Creators can receive direct payments from consumers, engage in token-based micropayments, or even explore the world of NFTs (Non-Fungible Tokens) to sell unique digital assets.

4. **Censorship Resistance**: Decentralized platforms are often resistant to censorship, as content isn't hosted on centralized servers. This means that creators have greater freedom to express themselves without the risk of content takedowns.

5. **Enhanced User Engagement**: These platforms promote a direct connection between creators and their audiences. Users can engage with creators, provide feedback, and even influence content creation.

8.1.3 Examples of Decentralized Content Platforms

1. **Steemit**: Steemit is a blockchain-based social media platform where users are rewarded with cryptocurrency for their contributions. It allows content creators to earn tokens based on the popularity of their posts.

2. **LBRY**: LBRY is a decentralized digital library and content sharing platform that enables creators to publish their work in a censorship-resistant manner while also allowing them to monetize it.

3. **Audius**: Audius is a decentralized music-sharing and streaming platform that empowers artists by eliminating intermediaries, enabling artists to earn directly from their work.

4. **Hive**: Hive is a blockchain-based social media and blogging platform where content creators are rewarded with cryptocurrency based on the engagement their posts receive.

8.1.4 Challenges and Future Prospects

While decentralized content platforms offer immense potential, they also face challenges related to user adoption, scalability, and ensuring quality content. As we navigate through this chapter, we will explore these challenges and discuss how they might be addressed in the ever-evolving landscape of Web 3.0 content publishing.

The exploration of decentralized content platforms within Web 3.0 demonstrates a fundamental shift in content creation and distribution, where creators and consumers are at the forefront of the content ecosystem. By understanding these platforms, content creators and enthusiasts can tap into the innovative and decentralized opportunities that the future of content publishing holds.

8.2 Censorship Resistance: Empowering Free Expression in Web 3.0 Content Publishing

In this section we explore a core principle that is reshaping the digital content landscape - censorship resistance. In the era of Web 3.0, censorship resistance stands as a powerful pillar that empowers free expression, protects content creators, and ensures open access to information.

8.2.1 The Challenge of Censorship

Traditional web platforms and content publishing channels have long grappled with issues of censorship. Governments, centralized entities, and third-party intermediaries have often exercised control over what can be shared and accessed online. This practice, while sometimes necessary for maintaining order, can stifle freedom of expression and limit the dissemination of critical information.

8.2.2 Censorship Resistance in Web 3.0

Web 3.0 technologies, with their decentralized and blockchain-based foundations, offer an antidote to censorship. They achieve this by distributing content across a network of nodes, making it extremely difficult for any single entity to control or censor information. Here's how censorship resistance is achieved in Web 3.0:

1. **Decentralized Hosting**: Content is hosted on decentralized networks, rather than on a central server. This means there is no single point of failure that can be targeted for censorship.

2. **Immutable Record**: Blockchain technology, a key component of Web 3.0, ensures that once content is recorded on the blockchain, it becomes immutable. This immutability makes it practically impossible to alter or delete content.

3. **Peer-to-Peer Communication**: Many Web 3.0 platforms enable peer-to-peer communication, where content is shared directly between users. This direct sharing bypasses intermediaries who might censor or surveil the content.

8.2.3 Use Cases and Implications

1. **Press Freedom**: Censorship-resistant platforms offer a lifeline for journalists and media outlets in regions

where press freedom is restricted. They can publish and share information without the fear of censorship.

2. **Whistleblower Protection**: Individuals who wish to expose wrongdoing or share sensitive information can do so safely on platforms that guarantee censorship resistance.

3. **Political Activism**: In politically sensitive environments, activists can organize, communicate, and share their views without the risk of censorship.

4. **Unfiltered Information**: Users can access information and content without third-party filtering, allowing them to form their own opinions based on unfiltered data.

8.2.4 Challenges and Considerations

1. **Legality**: Censorship resistance, while valuable, also raises legal and ethical questions. How do we balance the need to protect free speech with the responsibility to prevent harmful content?

2. **Content Moderation**: Ensuring that harmful and illegal content is not proliferated on these platforms is a complex challenge.

3. **Network Scalability**: As these platforms gain popularity, ensuring the scalability and performance of decentralized networks becomes vital.

The discussion on censorship resistance in Web 3.0 content publishing serves as a reminder of the transformative power of decentralized technologies. It empowers individuals, fosters open discourse, and ensures the free flow of information in a digital age where the need for censorship-resistant platforms has never been more evident.

8.3 Content Monetization in Web 3.0: Revolutionizing How Creators Earn

In this subparagraph we explore an exciting facet of the digital content landscape - content monetization in the era of Web 3.0. The advent of Web 3.0, with its decentralized technologies and innovative applications, has brought about a paradigm shift in how creators can monetize their content.

8.3.1 The Challenge of Content Monetization

In the Web 2.0 era, content monetization primarily relied on advertising revenue and paywalls. Creators often had to share a significant portion of their earnings with intermediaries, such as advertising platforms or distribution channels. This model had limitations, including issues related to privacy, ad-blocking, and revenue sharing.

8.3.2 Web 3.0 Monetization Strategies

Web 3.0 technologies offer a range of exciting new monetization opportunities for content creators, authors, artists, and influencers. Here are key strategies and concepts:

1. **Microtransactions with Cryptocurrencies**: Web 3.0 introduces the concept of microtransactions, where users can make tiny payments in cryptocurrency for access to premium content or services. This enables creators to receive direct compensation for their work without intermediaries taking a substantial cut.

2. **Non-Fungible Tokens (NFTs)**: NFTs represent ownership of unique digital assets. Creators can tokenize their content, such as digital art, music, or collectibles, and sell them as NFTs. This introduces a new dimension to content ownership and monetization.

3. **Blockchain-Based Subscriptions**: Creators can offer subscription models where users pay a recurring fee in cryptocurrency to access exclusive content or services. Blockchain ensures transparency in subscription billing.

4. **Decentralized Autonomous Organizations (DAOs)**: Creators can form or join DAOs, which are decentralized entities governed by smart contracts. DAO members can collectively fund and support content creation, sharing the revenues among themselves and creators.

5. **Creator Tokens**: Some platforms allow creators to launch their own tokens. These tokens can be traded and can accrue value as the creator's popularity and content offerings grow.

6. **Direct Fan Support**: Web 3.0 platforms enable direct communication between creators and their fans. Fans can offer support through microdonations or subscriptions, fostering a stronger creator-fan relationship.

8.3.3 Real-World Examples

1. **NFT Art Sales**: Artists like Beeple have sold digital art as NFTs for millions of dollars, revolutionizing the art industry.

2. **Blockchain-Based Streaming**: Platforms like Audius use blockchain to empower musicians by allowing them to retain more of their earnings from music streaming.

3. **Cryptocurrency-Based Paywalls**: Some news websites offer premium content accessible only to subscribers who pay in cryptocurrency.

8.3.4 Challenges and Considerations

1. **User Adoption**: Widespread adoption of cryptocurrency and Web 3.0 platforms is still evolving.

2. **Content Quality**: As creators directly monetize their content, ensuring high-quality and valuable content becomes paramount.

3. **Regulatory Compliance**: The evolving landscape of cryptocurrency regulation needs to be navigated.

The exploration of content monetization in Web 3.0 showcases how creators can take greater control of their work and finances. It's a testament to the transformative potential of decentralized technologies, fostering a more equitable and direct relationship between creators and their audiences.

8.4 Intellectual Property on the Blockchain: Safeguarding Creative Works in Web 3.0

Within this section we delve into an exciting dimension of the digital landscape - the integration of intellectual property protection with blockchain technology. In the era of Web 3.0, where decentralization and transparency are paramount, blockchain offers a robust solution for safeguarding intellectual property rights.

8.4.1 The Challenge of Intellectual Property Protection

Throughout the Web 2.0 era, creators and content owners have grappled with the unauthorized use and distribution of their intellectual property. Copyright infringement, plagiarism, and unauthorized sharing have been persistent issues. Traditional systems for protecting intellectual property, while functional, often face limitations in terms of transparency and enforcement.

8.4.2 Web 3.0 Solutions

Web 3.0 technologies, particularly blockchain, offer innovative ways to address these challenges:

1. **Immutable Record**: Blockchain's primary advantage is its immutability. Once data is recorded on the blockchain, it becomes tamper-proof, providing a transparent and unchangeable history of ownership and usage.

2. **Smart Contracts**: Smart contracts on blockchain platforms can automate and enforce copyright agreements. These contracts can stipulate the terms of use and ensure that creators receive compensation for the use of their work.

3. **NFTs and Ownership Tokens**: Creators can tokenize their intellectual property as Non-Fungible Tokens (NFTs) or ownership tokens. These digital assets represent ownership and can be transferred with ease, providing a clear record of who owns the rights.

4. **Decentralized Copyright Registries**: Platforms like Ethereum Name Service (ENS) offer decentralized ways to register and verify copyright ownership. This registry ensures a permanent and verifiable record of ownership.

5. **Proof of Creation**: Blockchain technology can serve as a timestamp, providing indisputable proof of when a

work was created. This is valuable for establishing the originality of creative works.

8.4.3 Real-World Use Cases

1. **NFT Art Ownership**: Artists tokenize their digital art as NFTs, proving their ownership and enabling them to sell and license their works securely.

2. **Music Royalties**: Musicians can receive royalties through smart contracts, ensuring that they are compensated for every use of their music.

3. **Digital Publishing**: Authors can use blockchain to track and control the distribution of their digital books, receiving direct payments from readers.

8.4.4 Challenges and Considerations

1. **Regulatory Framework**: Intellectual property laws and blockchain technology need to align, and legal frameworks need to adapt.

2. **User Adoption**: Widespread adoption of blockchain for intellectual property protection is essential for its effectiveness.

3. **Interoperability**: Ensuring different blockchain platforms can interact and recognize intellectual property rights is a complex challenge.

The exploration of intellectual property on the blockchain in Web 3.0 showcases how this innovative technology is revolutionizing the way creators protect and monetize their work. It provides an unprecedented level of transparency and security, ultimately empowering content creators and intellectual property owners.

8.5 New Models of Content Distribution: Redefining Access and Ownership in Web 3.0

The chapter on "Web 3.0 and Content Publishing" delves into the transformative landscape of content distribution in the era of Web 3.0. Web 3.0 technologies are redefining how content is distributed, accessed, and owned, ushering in a new era of decentralization and inclusivity.

8.5.1 Challenges in Traditional Content Distribution

Traditional content distribution models often relied on centralized intermediaries, which came with limitations such as content control, access restrictions, and revenue sharing concerns. These centralized systems posed challenges to content creators and consumers alike.

8.5.2 Web 3.0 Content Distribution Models

Web 3.0 introduces innovative models that address these challenges:

1. **Decentralized Content Networks**: Content is distributed across decentralized networks of nodes,

eliminating single points of control and enhancing reliability. Users contribute their resources, such as bandwidth and storage, to host and distribute content.

2. **Peer-to-Peer (P2P) Sharing**: Web 3.0 platforms facilitate direct P2P sharing of content, allowing users to access and share content without intermediaries. This ensures open access and fosters a sense of ownership among users.

3. **Tokenized Ownership**: Content creators can tokenize their work, transforming it into NFTs or ownership tokens. This not only proves ownership but also allows creators to earn royalties whenever their content is accessed or shared.

4. **Content DAOs**: Decentralized Autonomous Organizations (DAOs) are formed by content creators and users, allowing them to collectively manage and distribute content. Revenue generated is shared among participants.

5. **Blockchain-based Subscriptions**: Users can pay for content using cryptocurrencies through subscription models. Blockchain ensures transparency in subscription billing.

8.5.3 Real-World Examples

1. **BitTorrent**: A P2P protocol for file sharing, BitTorrent allows users to share and distribute large files without central servers.

2. **IPFS (InterPlanetary File System)**: IPFS is a decentralized and peer-to-peer protocol that enables users to share and access content through a distributed network.

3. **Audius**: Audius is a blockchain-based music streaming platform that empowers musicians to share and monetize their music directly with fans.

8.5.4 Challenges and Considerations

1. **Scalability**: As Web 3.0 content distribution platforms gain popularity, ensuring network scalability and performance is crucial.

2. **Content Quality**: Maintaining high-quality content and preventing the spread of harmful or illegal content remains a priority.

3. **User Adoption**: Widespread adoption of Web 3.0 content distribution platforms is a key factor in their success.

The exploration of new models of content distribution in Web 3.0 underscores the transformation of the digital content landscape. It emphasizes decentralized and community-driven approaches that prioritize open access, ownership, and the empowerment of content creators and consumers alike.

Chapter 9: Navigating the Path to Web 3.0: Challenges and Barriers

In the ever-evolving journey towards Web 3.0 and the broader adoption of decentralized technologies, it is imperative to acknowledge the obstacles, complexities, and barriers that lie along the path. The chapter on "Challenges and Barriers" in this book offers a critical examination of the hurdles that must be overcome to realize the full potential of Web 3.0 and decentralized technologies.

9.1 Scalability Issues: The Struggle to Expand Web 3.0

In the relentless pursuit of Web 3.0, one of the most formidable barriers encountered on this journey is the formidable challenge of scalability. The chapter on "Challenges and Barriers" in this book delves into the critical issue of scalability within the context of Web 3.0 and decentralized technologies.

9.1.1 The Grand Vision of Web 3.0

Web 3.0 envisions an internet that is not only decentralized and user-centric but also capable of handling a massive influx of data, transactions, and user interactions. This vision is promising, but it places unprecedented demands on the underlying technologies.

9.1.2 Key Scalability Issues

1. **Blockchain Congestion**: Blockchain technology, a cornerstone of Web 3.0, often faces congestion and slow transaction speeds as it struggles to accommodate the increasing number of users and transactions.

2. **Data Storage**: Decentralized systems require extensive data storage capabilities, and scaling this to match demand is a significant challenge.

3. **Interoperability**: As Web 3.0 embraces multiple blockchain networks and decentralized applications, ensuring they can communicate and operate cohesively at scale becomes a complex technical challenge.

4. **Energy Efficiency**: The energy consumption of some blockchain networks, like Bitcoin, raises concerns about sustainability and environmental impact.

5. **User Experience**: Slow transaction times and high fees can deter users from adopting decentralized technologies.

6. **Smart Contracts**: The execution of complex smart contracts on a blockchain can be resource-intensive and slow.

9.1.3 Strategies and Solutions

The chapter explores various strategies and innovative solutions that are being employed to address scalability issues:

1. **Layer 2 Solutions**: Layer 2 solutions, such as the Lightning Network for Bitcoin and sidechains, aim to offload some of the transaction burden from the main blockchain, enhancing scalability.

2. **Sharding**: Sharding, a technique employed by blockchain platforms like Ethereum, partitions the network into smaller, more manageable pieces to improve scalability.

3. **Consensus Mechanisms**: Alternative consensus mechanisms, like Proof of Stake (PoS), are more energy-efficient and scalable compared to traditional Proof of Work (PoW) systems.

4. **Cross-Chain Compatibility**: Solutions for inter-blockchain operability, such as Polkadot, aim to create a network of interconnected blockchains, enabling seamless data and asset transfer.

5. **Research and Development**: Ongoing research in the field of blockchain and decentralized technology is dedicated to finding innovative approaches to scalability.

9.1.4 Collaboration and Innovation

Web 3.0 enthusiasts, developers, and organizations are actively collaborating to find scalable solutions. The chapter highlights the importance of collective efforts and innovative thinking to overcome scalability challenges, as they stand as a fundamental hurdle to realizing the ambitious vision of Web 3.0.

Understanding the intricacies of scalability issues is essential for anyone venturing into the realm of Web 3.0 and decentralized technologies. The path to a scalable, decentralized future is challenging, but it is one that holds great promise and potential.

9.2 Regulatory and Legal Challenges: Navigating the Regulatory Landscape of Web 3.0

In the pursuit of Web 3.0 and the widespread adoption of decentralized technologies, an intricate web of regulatory and legal challenges arises. The chapter on "Challenges and Barriers" in this book sheds light on the complex landscape of regulations that intersect with the transformative potential of Web 3.0.

9.2.1 The Vision of a Decentralized Web

Web 3.0 envisions an internet free from central authorities and intermediaries. It promotes decentralization, transparency, and user sovereignty. However, as these technologies gain momentum, they encounter a dynamic and evolving regulatory environment.

9.2.2 Key Regulatory and Legal Challenges

1. **Cryptocurrency Regulation**: The regulation of cryptocurrencies, a fundamental component of Web 3.0, varies significantly across countries. Issues of taxation, anti-money laundering (AML), and know-your-customer (KYC) requirements create hurdles for users and businesses.

2. **Security Token Regulation**: Security tokens represent ownership or rights to assets, and their issuance and trading are subject to securities regulations, adding complexity to blockchain-based ventures.

3. **Smart Contract Legality**: The enforceability and legal status of smart contracts, which automatically execute actions on blockchain networks, remain a point of contention.

4. **Data Privacy**: Decentralized applications often handle personal data, raising concerns about compliance with data protection laws like GDPR.

5. **Cross-Border Transactions**: The global nature of blockchain and decentralized technologies complicates the jurisdictional and cross-border aspects of regulation.

6. **Consumer Protection**: Ensuring the safety and protection of consumers and investors in the decentralized space is a challenge for regulators.

7. **Intellectual Property**: Web 3.0's embrace of digital assets and tokenization prompts questions about the regulation of intellectual property rights.

9.2.3 Navigating the Regulatory Landscape

The chapter explores how Web 3.0 enthusiasts, entrepreneurs, and organizations are navigating this intricate regulatory landscape:

1. **Compliance and Dialogue**: Engaging with regulators and policymakers to promote compliance and understanding is a proactive approach.

2. **Regulatory Sandboxes**: Some regions offer regulatory sandboxes where innovative blockchain and fintech projects can operate under controlled conditions to develop and prove their concepts.

3. **Self-Regulation**: Some industries have opted for self-regulation through industry associations and best practices.

4. **Legal Frameworks**: Legal experts and firms specializing in blockchain and decentralized technologies are working on creating legal frameworks to address specific challenges.

9.2.4 The Need for Collaboration

Web 3.0's vision of decentralization challenges existing regulatory paradigms. The chapter highlights the importance of collaboration between the Web 3.0 community and regulatory bodies to create an environment that fosters innovation while ensuring user protection.

As Web 3.0 continues to evolve, a harmonious relationship between technological progress and regulatory compliance is crucial. Understanding the intricate web of regulatory and legal challenges is fundamental to successfully navigating the path toward a decentralized and user-centric digital future.

9.3 User Adoption Hurdles: Bridging the Gap to Web 3.0

The journey toward Web 3.0 and the broader adoption of decentralized technologies is marked by an array of hurdles and complexities, with one of the most significant being the challenge of user adoption. The chapter on "Challenges and Barriers" in this book delves into the pivotal issue of user adoption within the context of Web 3.0 and decentralized technologies.

9.3.1 The Vision of User-Centric Web 3.0

Web 3.0 aspires to put users in control of their digital experiences, offering them greater security, privacy, and autonomy over their online activities. This vision is compelling, but it necessitates a fundamental shift in user behavior and the adoption of new technologies and practices.

9.3.2 Key User Adoption Hurdles

1. **Complexity of Decentralized Technologies**: Decentralized technologies often come with a steep learning curve, making it challenging for non-technical users to understand and utilize them effectively.

2. **Change in User Behavior**: Encouraging users to shift from centralized platforms they are accustomed to and trust to new, decentralized alternatives is a significant challenge.

3. **Wallet and Key Management**: Managing cryptographic keys and wallets, a fundamental aspect of using decentralized applications, can be intimidating for non-technical users.

4. **Scalability and User Experience**: Some decentralized platforms face issues related to slow transaction times and high fees, which can deter users accustomed to faster and cheaper centralized alternatives.

5. **Lack of Awareness**: Many potential users are not aware of the benefits of Web 3.0 and decentralized

technologies, necessitating education and awareness campaigns.

9.3.3 Strategies for User Adoption

The chapter explores various strategies and best practices employed to address user adoption hurdles:

1. **User-Friendly Interfaces**: Developing intuitive and user-friendly interfaces for decentralized applications and services is a critical step in mitigating the complexity barrier.

2. **Education and Training**: Educating users about the benefits of decentralized technologies and providing training resources to help them navigate this new landscape.

3. **Incentives and Rewards**: Offering incentives, such as tokens or rewards, can motivate users to explore and adopt decentralized platforms.

4. **Community Building**: Building communities around decentralized projects helps users share knowledge and experiences.

5. **Interoperability**: Ensuring that decentralized applications can work together seamlessly makes it easier for users to transition between platforms.

9.3.4 The Role of Collaboration

User adoption challenges are not to be underestimated, but they are challenges that can be surmounted through collaboration and collective effort. The Web 3.0 community, developers, and organizations must work together to make the transition as smooth and user-friendly as possible.

Understanding the intricacies of user adoption hurdles is essential for those striving to accelerate the adoption of Web 3.0 and decentralized technologies. The path to a user-centric, decentralized future is a challenging one, but it is also one filled with promise and opportunities for innovation and empowerment.

9.4 Interoperability and Standards: Bridging the Web 3.0 Divide

In the journey towards Web 3.0 and the widespread adoption of decentralized technologies, one of the paramount challenges is interoperability and the need for established standards. The chapter on "Challenges and Barriers" in this book investigates the significance of interoperability and standards within the context of Web 3.0.

9.4.1 The Vision of Seamless Integration

Web 3.0 envisions an internet that is decentralized, user-centric, and capable of seamlessly integrating a multitude of technologies, applications, and services. Achieving this vision hinges on the ability of these various components to communicate and work cohesively together.

9.4.2 Key Interoperability and Standards Challenges

1. **Diverse Blockchain Ecosystem**: The proliferation of blockchain platforms and decentralized applications (DApps) often operates in silos, making it challenging for them to interoperate.

2. **Fragmented Decentralized Services**: Decentralized services, from identity management to data storage, need to communicate effectively, yet they often lack standardized protocols.

3. **User Experience**: Inconsistencies in user experience across various decentralized platforms can deter users from transitioning from familiar centralized systems.

4. **Cross-Chain Compatibility**: Web 3.0 envisions a future where different blockchain networks can interact seamlessly, but achieving this is a technical challenge.

5. **Regulatory Requirements**: Interoperability must also align with various regulatory and compliance standards, which differ from one jurisdiction to another.

9.4.3 Strategies for Interoperability and Standards

The chapter explores strategies and best practices to tackle interoperability challenges and foster the establishment of standards:

1. **Blockchain Interoperability Protocols**: Solutions like Polkadot and Cosmos aim to connect various blockchains to enable cross-chain communication and asset transfer.

2. **Cross-Industry Collaboration**: Industry consortia and collaborative initiatives are developing standards and protocols to foster interoperability in sectors like finance and supply chain.

3. **Open Source Development**: Embracing open source principles enables a community-driven effort to create interoperable technologies and standards.

4. **Regulatory Engagement**: Engaging with regulatory bodies to establish standardized compliance requirements can harmonize interoperability efforts.

5. **Education and Awareness**: Promoting awareness of the importance of interoperability and standards encourages developers and organizations to prioritize these issues.

9.4.4 The Role of Collaboration

Interoperability and standards are complex and multifaceted challenges, but they are ones that can be overcome through collaboration. The Web 3.0 community, blockchain developers, and organizations must work together to create an environment where systems can communicate seamlessly and standards can be established.

Understanding the intricacies of interoperability and standards is paramount for those involved in the development and adoption of Web 3.0 and decentralized technologies. The path to a truly interoperable, user-centric, and decentralized future is challenging, but it is also one filled with boundless opportunities for innovation and advancement.

9.5 Governance in Decentralized Systems: A Key Challenge on the Path to Web 3.0

In the pursuit of Web 3.0 and the broader adoption of decentralized technologies, governance stands as a formidable challenge and a vital piece of the puzzle. The chapter on "Challenges and Barriers" in this book explores the intricate dynamics of governance within the context of Web 3.0.

9.5.1 The Vision of Decentralization and Self-Governance

Web 3.0 envisions an internet where power is distributed, putting control in the hands of the community. While the goal is decentralization, the question of how decentralized systems should be governed remains a complex and evolving issue.

9.5.2 Key Governance Challenges

1. **Decision-Making Processes**: In decentralized systems, decisions must be made collectively, often through consensus mechanisms. Determining how decisions are reached and who gets to participate is an ongoing challenge.

2. **Token Holder Influence**: Many decentralized platforms rely on token-based governance, where the more tokens you hold, the more influence you have. Balancing this influence and preventing centralization is a constant struggle.

3. **Legal Compliance**: Governance decisions must often align with legal and regulatory requirements, adding complexity to the decision-making process.

4. **Community Engagement**: Ensuring that the community, including both technical and non-technical users, is engaged in governance processes is a challenge.

5. **Upgrades and Forks**: Decentralized platforms must navigate how upgrades and forks are executed while minimizing disruption.

9.5.3 Strategies for Governance in Decentralized Systems

The chapter delves into strategies and best practices for addressing governance challenges:

1. **On-Chain Governance Tools**: The use of on-chain governance tools allows token holders to participate in decision-making directly within the blockchain.

2. **Decentralized Autonomous Organizations (DAOs)**: DAOs are entities that rely on smart contracts and code to automate decision-making, offering a potential solution to governance challenges.

3. **Transparency and Accountability**: Openly documenting governance decisions and ensuring accountability can build trust within the community.

4. **Legal and Regulatory Experts**: Engaging with legal and regulatory experts to ensure governance decisions comply with local laws is essential.

5. **Education and Awareness**: Educating the community about governance processes and their significance can encourage active participation.

9.5.4 The Role of Collaboration

Governance in decentralized systems is a multifaceted challenge, and it requires collaboration between developers, platform users, and experts in various fields to establish effective, fair, and transparent governance models. Striking a balance between decentralization and the need for structure and decision-making processes is a critical endeavor.

Understanding the complexities of governance in decentralized systems is essential for those striving to navigate the path to a more decentralized, user-centric digital future. While the challenges are significant, they are also opportunities to shape governance in ways that align with the principles of Web 3.0.

Chapter 10: The Future of Web 3.0: Shaping a Decentralized Digital Landscape

As we delve into the chapter on "The Future of Web 3.0: Shaping a Decentralized Digital Landscape" we stand at a pivotal moment in the evolution of the internet. Web 3.0 and decentralized technologies have emerged as the vanguards of a profound transformation, promising to reshape the digital landscape as we know it.

Web 3.0: A Vision Unfolding

Web 3.0 is not just an iteration but a revolution in the making. It envisions a future where the internet is decentralized, empowering users and enabling trust and security through cryptographic principles. It embodies a shift from centralization and control to openness, transparency, and community-driven innovation.

Unraveling the Potential

The future of Web 3.0 holds a tapestry of possibilities. In this chapter, we will explore the paths that lie ahead, the technologies that will play pivotal roles, and the impact that these changes will have on individuals, businesses, and societies.

10.1 Anticipated Technological Advances: Pioneering the Future of Web 3.0

In our exploration of "The Future of Web 3.0," it's essential to peer into the crystal ball of technology, foreseeing the advances that will shape this decentralized digital landscape. The future of Web 3.0 is not only about reimagining the present but also about inventing the innovations of tomorrow.

10.1.1 Interconnected Blockchains

The future of Web 3.0 hinges on seamless integration among diverse blockchains. Cross-chain compatibility, often dubbed "blockchain interoperability," is a technological leap that will enable these separate networks to communicate and transact effortlessly. Protocols like Polkadot and Cosmos are pioneering this vision.

10.1.2 Scalability Solutions

Scalability remains a core issue. As Web 3.0 seeks mass adoption, blockchain networks must evolve to handle a growing user base and transaction load. Layer 2 solutions, like the Lightning Network for Bitcoin and the myriad Ethereum Layer 2 scaling solutions, are destined to refine this landscape.

10.1.3 Advanced Consensus Mechanisms

Proof of Stake (PoS) and Delegated Proof of Stake (DPoS) consensus mechanisms will gain prominence. These more eco-friendly, efficient, and democratic mechanisms are anticipated to replace energy-intensive Proof of Work (PoW) systems in various blockchain networks.

10.1.4 Quantum-Resistant Cryptography

The advent of quantum computing poses a threat to contemporary cryptographic methods. Quantum-resistant cryptography will become increasingly vital to safeguard the decentralized web against emerging quantum threats.

10.1.5 Enhanced Privacy Technologies

Privacy coins and privacy-enhancing technologies, such as zero-knowledge proofs, will play a pivotal role in preserving user data protection. The future of Web 3.0 emphasizes privacy as a fundamental right.

10.1.6 Decentralized Storage Solutions

In the era of Web 3.0, storage will not only be decentralized but also more secure and efficient. Technologies like IPFS (InterPlanetary File System) and Swarm are poised to alter the way data is stored and retrieved.

10.1.7 AI and Machine Learning Integration

Web 3.0 will witness the infusion of AI and machine learning into decentralized applications, enabling intelligent, automated, and personalized user experiences.

10.1.8 User-Friendly Wallets and Interfaces

A user-centric Web 3.0 demands more user-friendly wallets and interfaces, reducing the barriers to entry and enhancing the overall experience for individuals new to decentralized technologies.

10.1.9 Internet of Things (IoT) Integration

The marriage of Web 3.0 and IoT will create a world of interconnected, autonomous devices with blockchain technology ensuring secure and transparent communication between them.

10.1.10 Advancements in Decentralized Identity

Self-sovereign identity solutions will flourish, enabling individuals to have more control over their personal data and digital identity. This will be a cornerstone of the Web 3.0 user experience.

10.1.11 Navigating the Uncharted Territories

The future of Web 3.0 is brimming with innovation and promise. Yet, it also comes with challenges and uncertainties. Developers, businesses, and users alike will navigate this terrain, pioneering new technologies, and pushing the boundaries of what's possible in a decentralized digital world.

As we peer into the future, it's essential to remember that the destiny of Web 3.0 is not etched in stone; rather, it's a tapestry that we collectively weave with technological breakthroughs, visionary thinking, and a shared commitment to the principles of decentralization, trust, and user empowerment. The promise of Web 3.0 is a future that beckons us to explore, innovate, and shape the decentralized digital landscape.

10.2 Industry and Business Transformation: Navigating Web 3.0's Disruptive Wave

In the journey into "The Future of Web 3.0," it becomes evident that the transformative power of this decentralized digital landscape extends far beyond technology. The business and industrial realms are poised for profound changes that will reshape traditional paradigms.

10.2.1 Decentralized Finance (DeFi) and Traditional Finance

Web 3.0's financial ecosystem, built on blockchain technology, is challenging the conventional financial world. DeFi, with its decentralized lending, borrowing, and trading, presents an alternative that empowers individuals and reduces reliance on centralized financial institutions.

10.2.2 Supply Chain Revolution

Blockchain technology enables end-to-end traceability and transparency in supply chains. This revolutionizes how businesses track the movement of goods, verify authenticity, and respond to challenges, such as recalls or counterfeit products.

10.2.3 Content Creation and Distribution

Web 3.0 introduces innovative models for content creation and distribution. Creators can be directly rewarded through microtransactions and token economies, reducing the influence of intermediaries.

10.2.4 Intellectual Property and Royalties

The blockchain provides a transparent and immutable ledger for tracking intellectual property rights and royalties. This has the potential to revolutionize how artists, writers, and content creators are compensated for their work.

10.2.5 Decentralized Autonomous Organizations (DAOs)

Businesses can now operate as DAOs, making decisions using smart contracts and consensus mechanisms. This reduces the need for traditional hierarchical structures and intermediaries.

10.2.6 Digital Identity Verification

Web 3.0's self-sovereign identity solutions allow businesses to verify users' identities without collecting and storing personal data, improving security and privacy.

10.2.7 Disruption in Traditional Advertising

Decentralized advertising platforms using blockchain technology provide a more transparent and efficient way for businesses to advertise, eliminating ad fraud and middlemen.

10.2.8 Smart Contracts in Legal Services

Smart contracts are automating legal processes, reducing the need for traditional legal intermediaries and streamlining contract execution.

10.2.9 Healthcare and Data Security

Web 3.0 enhances the security of healthcare data through blockchain-based patient records and enables more efficient sharing of medical information.

10.2.10 Decentralized Autonomous Organizations (DAOs)

Businesses can now operate as DAOs, making decisions using smart contracts and consensus mechanisms. This reduces the need for traditional hierarchical structures and intermediaries.

10.2.11 Embracing the New Paradigm

The transition to Web 3.0 presents both challenges and opportunities. Businesses and industries must adapt to this decentralized landscape, embracing transparency, security, and user empowerment. Those who do so will be at the forefront of this transformative wave, while those who resist may face obsolescence.

As we peer into the future of industry and business in Web 3.0, the key takeaway is that innovation, agility, and a willingness to explore and adapt to new paradigms will be the driving forces for success. In this evolving digital landscape, the ability to harness the potential of decentralized technologies will determine which businesses and industries thrive in the Web 3.0 era.

10.3 The Societal Impact of Web 3.0: Navigating a New Social Order

As we delve into "The Future of Web 3.0" it becomes clear that the impact of this decentralized digital landscape extends far beyond technology and business—it reaches into the very fabric of society. Web 3.0 is poised to instigate transformative societal changes that will redefine the way we interact, communicate, and govern ourselves.

10.3.1 Redefining Digital Identity

Web 3.0 heralds a new era of digital identity. Self-sovereign identity solutions empower individuals to control their personal data, reducing the influence of tech giants and promoting privacy.

10.3.2 Democratized Information

Decentralized content platforms challenge the centralized control of information. Censorship-resistant platforms ensure that a broader spectrum of voices can be heard, fostering a more diverse and inclusive digital discourse.

10.3.3 Economic Empowerment

The financial ecosystem of Web 3.0, characterized by DeFi, cryptocurrencies, and token economies, offers economic empowerment to individuals worldwide, particularly in regions with limited access to traditional financial services.

10.3.4 Trust in Technology

Blockchain's transparent and tamper-resistant nature rebuilds trust in digital systems. Trust in technology, once eroded by privacy concerns and data breaches, is restored, leading to increased reliance on digital tools for essential services.

10.3.5 Decentralized Governance

Web 3.0 facilitates new models of governance through DAOs and consensus mechanisms. This could redefine the social contract, enabling more direct participation in decision-making and reducing the influence of centralized authorities.

10.3.6 Personalized and Private Experiences

AI and machine learning integrated into Web 3.0 provide personalized user experiences while preserving user privacy. Individuals receive tailored services without sacrificing their personal data.

10.3.7 Global Collaboration

The decentralized nature of Web 3.0 fosters global collaboration. Cross-border projects, humanitarian efforts, and collaborative innovations become more accessible.

10.3.8 Environmental Sustainability

The shift from energy-intensive Proof of Work (PoW) to energy-efficient Proof of Stake (PoS) and eco-friendly consensus mechanisms aligns with global efforts to reduce the carbon footprint, contributing to a more sustainable future.

10.3.9 Bridging the Digital Divide

Web 3.0 technologies have the potential to bridge the digital divide, providing internet access, financial services, and digital identity to underserved populations, offering new opportunities for education and economic growth.

10.3.10 Evolving Social Norms

Web 3.0's impact on privacy, security, and digital empowerment will challenge and evolve societal norms and expectations regarding technology, data ownership, and individual rights.

10.3.11 Navigating Societal Transformations

The societal impact of Web 3.0 is profound, presenting an array of possibilities and challenges. As society navigates this transformation, it's essential to collectively shape a future that embraces the principles of decentralization, trust, and user empowerment. The journey into Web 3.0 extends beyond technology—it's a reimagining of our digital world and our roles within it. It calls for a careful exploration of the societal dynamics that will define our future in this new digital landscape.

10.4 Preparing for a Decentralized Future: Navigating the Transition to Web 3.0

As we embark on the journey towards "The Future of Web 3.0" it is imperative to recognize that the decentralized digital landscape will require a fundamental shift in how we prepare, adapt, and thrive in this transformative era. To navigate this transition effectively, individuals, organizations, and societies must take proactive steps to embrace Web 3.0's potential while addressing the associated challenges.

10.4.1 Digital Literacy and Education

To succeed in Web 3.0, individuals must acquire digital literacy skills that encompass blockchain technology, cryptocurrencies, decentralized applications (DApps), and smart contracts. Educational institutions and training programs should adapt to provide this essential knowledge.

10.4.2 User-Centric Data Management

Empowering individuals with control over their digital identities and data is pivotal. Innovations in decentralized identity and privacy solutions enable individuals to manage their personal information securely. Society must recognize the value of these solutions and adopt them widely.

10.4.3 Regulatory Frameworks

Governments and regulatory bodies need to create adaptive and supportive frameworks that balance innovation with security. These frameworks should encourage the development of decentralized technologies while addressing potential risks and ensuring compliance with the law.

10.4.4 Business Adaptation

Enterprises must adapt to the decentralized landscape, exploring ways to incorporate blockchain, smart contracts, and decentralized finance (DeFi) into their operations. This involves a reevaluation of business models, processes, and partnerships.

10.4.5 Environmental Responsibility

Web 3.0's transition to more energy-efficient consensus mechanisms should be met with a commitment to environmental responsibility. The industry must minimize its carbon footprint and contribute to a more sustainable digital future.

10.4.6 Decentralized Governance

Society should explore decentralized governance models through DAOs and consensus mechanisms. This shift necessitates a reimagining of how decisions are made and policies are enacted, with the goal of reducing centralization and increasing participation.

10.4.7 Bridging the Digital Divide

Efforts should focus on bridging the digital divide by extending access to Web 3.0 technologies, especially in underserved regions. Initiatives can include internet access, digital education, and financial inclusion programs.

10.4.8 Ethical Considerations

As Web 3.0 empowers individuals with more control over their digital lives, it raises ethical considerations. Discussions on ethics in technology, data ownership, and privacy should guide the development of this decentralized era.

10.4.9 Interdisciplinary Collaboration

Web 3.0's multifaceted nature necessitates interdisciplinary collaboration. Technologists, policymakers, social scientists, and ethicists should work together to shape a future that respects human rights and values.

10.4.10 Preparedness for Paradigm Shifts

Preparing for a decentralized future means acknowledging that societal and technological paradigms are shifting. It requires an open mindset and a willingness to adapt, learn, and explore the transformative potential of Web 3.0.

The transition to a decentralized future is not without its challenges, but it also offers a world of opportunities. Success in this new digital landscape depends on our collective preparedness, adaptability, and the decisions we make today. By embracing the principles of decentralization, user empowerment, and trust in technology, we can navigate this transformation with confidence and shape a future that reflects our aspirations and values.

10.5 Conclusion and Call to Action: Shaping the Web 3.0 Future

In concluding our journey through the landscape of Web 3.0 and decentralized technologies, we stand at the precipice of a new digital era. The path ahead is both exciting and challenging, marked by unprecedented opportunities and uncharted territories. As we reflect on the transformative potential of Web 3.0, it is essential to consider the role we each play in shaping this decentralized future.

10.5.1 Embracing the Potential

Web 3.0 offers a world where individuals have greater control over their digital lives, where trust is restored in technology, and where global collaboration knows no boundaries. It provides solutions to problems that have long plagued the centralized web and opens doors to innovations that can improve lives worldwide.

10.5.2 Addressing the Challenges

However, the journey to Web 3.0 is not without its hurdles. Scalability, regulatory concerns, user adoption, and interoperability are challenges that demand our collective attention. These are the obstacles we must overcome to unlock the full potential of decentralization.

10.5.3 A Call to Action

It's no longer enough to be a passive observer in this transformation. The call to action is clear:

1. **Educate Yourself:** Embrace digital literacy and seek to understand the technologies that underpin Web 3.0. Explore blockchain, cryptocurrencies, and decentralized applications to empower yourself in this decentralized landscape.

2. **Advocate for Change:** Be an advocate for regulatory frameworks that foster innovation while ensuring safety and security. Engage with policymakers and stakeholders to shape a regulatory environment that enables decentralized technologies to flourish.

3. **Drive Business Transformation:** If you are part of the business world, drive innovation within your organization. Explore how blockchain, smart contracts, and DeFi can enhance your operations and create new value for your customers.

4. **Promote Ethical Practices:** Champion ethical considerations in technology, data privacy, and digital identity. Act in ways that respect user rights and prioritize security.

5. **Collaborate Across Disciplines:** The decentralized future requires interdisciplinary collaboration. Engage with professionals from various backgrounds to address the multifaceted challenges and opportunities presented by Web 3.0.

6. **Stay Informed:** Keep up-to-date with the latest developments in the Web 3.0 space. The technology is evolving rapidly, and staying informed is essential to making informed decisions.

10.5.4 A Future Shaped by Us

The future of Web 3.0 is not predetermined; it is a future that we collectively shape through our actions, decisions, and innovations. It is a future where the decentralized internet aligns with our values of trust, user empowerment, and inclusivity.

As we embark on this journey, let us remember that the power to transform the digital landscape lies within each of us. The call to action is an invitation to be active participants in the creation of a decentralized future that reflects our aspirations and ideals. Together, we can shape a Web 3.0 that benefits humanity as a whole and paves the way for a more inclusive, secure, and innovative digital world.

11 Glossary of Terms: Web 3.0 and Decentralized Technologies

1. Blockchain: A distributed ledger technology that records transactions across multiple computers in a way that ensures security, transparency, and immutability.

2. Cryptocurrency: Digital or virtual currencies that use cryptography for security. Examples include Bitcoin, Ethereum, and Litecoin.

3. Decentralized Applications (DApps): Applications built on blockchain or decentralized networks that operate without a central authority.

4. Smart Contracts: Self-executing contracts with the terms of the agreement between buyer and seller written into code, automatically executing when predefined conditions are met.

5. Web 3.0: The next evolution of the internet, characterized by decentralization, user empowerment, and the use of technologies like blockchain and AI to enable a more secure and trust-based digital ecosystem.

6. DeFi (Decentralized Finance): Financial services, such as lending, borrowing, and trading, built on blockchain and decentralized platforms, enabling peer-to-peer transactions without traditional intermediaries.

7. DAO (Decentralized Autonomous Organization): An organization represented by rules encoded as a computer program that is transparent, controlled by the organization members, and not influenced by a central government.

8. IPFS (InterPlanetary File System): A protocol and network designed to create a content-addressable, peer-to-peer method of storing and sharing hypermedia in a distributed file system.

9. Consensus Mechanisms: Protocols used in blockchain to achieve agreement among nodes on a single data value. Examples include Proof of Work (PoW) and Proof of Stake (PoS).

10. Digital Identity: The set of information about an individual, organization, or device, represented in a digital format and used for various online activities and transactions.

11. Self-Sovereign Identity: An individual's ownership and control over their personal data and identity, reducing reliance on centralized entities for identity verification.

12. Decentralized Domain Name Systems (DDNS): Systems that enable domain name registration and management without reliance on a centralized authority, enhancing online security and reducing censorship.

13. Cryptography: The practice of secure communication techniques that protect information by transforming it into an unreadable format, which can only be reversed with the correct decryption key.

14. Smart Property: Physical or digital assets that are uniquely identifiable, have ownership history, and are equipped with the ability to self-execute smart contracts.

15. NFT (Non-Fungible Token): A unique digital asset representing ownership or proof of authenticity of a specific item or piece of content, often used in art, gaming, and collectibles.

16. DAO Governance Tokens: Tokens that grant holders the ability to vote on proposals and decisions within a decentralized autonomous organization.

17. Web 3.0 Interoperability: The ability of various blockchain and decentralized technologies to work together seamlessly, allowing data and assets to flow between different platforms.

18. Regulatory Sandbox: A controlled environment where startups and businesses can test innovative products, services, or business models without facing full regulatory requirements.

19. Peer-to-Peer (P2P): A decentralized network model where participants interact directly with one another without the need for a central server or intermediary.

20. Digital Wallet: A software or hardware tool that stores the private and public keys needed to interact with blockchain networks and manage cryptocurrencies.

21. Censorship Resistance: The ability of a system or technology to resist efforts to suppress, manipulate, or control information or transactions.

22. Web 3.0 Ecosystem: The interconnected web of decentralized technologies, applications, and platforms that form the foundation of the new internet era.

23. Identity Verification: The process of confirming an individual's or entity's identity through various means, often for security, compliance, or access purposes.

24. Cross-Border Transactions: Transactions that occur between individuals, businesses, or entities located in different countries, often facilitated by decentralized finance (DeFi) platforms.

25. Trustless Transactions: Transactions that do not require trust in a central authority or intermediary, as they are verified and executed automatically by smart contracts or blockchain technology.

26. Digital Inclusion: Efforts to ensure that all individuals, regardless of location or socioeconomic status, have equal access to and benefit from the opportunities provided by Web 3.0 technologies.

12 References and Further Reading

In the process of exploring the world of Web 3.0 and decentralized technologies, you've embarked on a journey that's ever-evolving. The following references and further reading materials are your guide to deepening your understanding, keeping up with the latest developments, and exploring related topics in more detail.

12.1 Books

1. "Mastering Bitcoin: Unlocking Digital Cryptocurrencies" by Andreas M. Antonopoulos

    - A comprehensive guide to understanding the fundamentals of Bitcoin and blockchain technology.

2. "The Internet of Money" by Andreas M. Antonopoulos

    - A collection of talks that demystify cryptocurrencies and their potential impact.

3. "Blockchain Basics: A Non-Technical Introduction in 25 Steps" by Daniel Drescher

    - A beginner-friendly introduction to the principles of blockchain technology.

4. "Decentralized Applications: Harnessing Bitcoin's Blockchain Technology" by Siraj Raval

    - A practical guide to building decentralized applications (DApps) on blockchain platforms.

5. "The Basics of Bitcoins and Blockchains" by Antony Lewis

- An accessible introduction to blockchain technology, cryptocurrencies, and their use cases.

12.2 Online Resources

6. CryptoCompare (https://www.cryptocompare.com/)

    - A comprehensive cryptocurrency data platform with real-time and historical data on cryptocurrencies.

7. Ethereum's Official Documentation (https://ethereum.org/en/developers/docs/)

    - The official resource for learning about Ethereum, smart contracts, and DApps development.

8. Coindesk (https://www.coindesk.com/)

    - A leading cryptocurrency news outlet providing the latest news, analysis, and insights.

9. The Defiant (https://thedefiant.io/)

    - A newsletter and website focused on decentralized finance (DeFi) and the intersection of blockchain and finance.

12.3 Academic Journals and Papers

10. "Bitcoin: A Peer-to-Peer Electronic Cash System" by Satoshi Nakamoto

    - The original Bitcoin whitepaper that laid the foundation for the entire blockchain ecosystem.

11. "Ethereum: A Secure Decentralized Generalized Transaction Ledger" by Vitalik Buterin

    - The whitepaper that introduced Ethereum, the smart contract platform.

12. "The Meaning of Decentralization" by Vitalik Buterin

    - An exploration of the concept of decentralization in the context of cryptocurrencies and blockchain technology.

12.4 Forums and Communities

13. Stack Exchange - Bitcoin (https://bitcoin.stackexchange.com/)

    - A Q&A community for Bitcoin enthusiasts and developers.

14. Ethereum Stack Exchange (https://ethereum.stackexchange.com/)

- A similar community focused on Ethereum and smart contract development.

15. [Crypto Twitter](https://www.coindesk.com/tag/crypto-twitter/)

- A vibrant source of real-time updates and discussions on the latest developments in the crypto and blockchain space.

These references and further reading materials are just the beginning of your journey into the world of Web 3.0 and decentralized technologies. Stay curious, stay informed, and continue exploring this transformative digital landscape. The future is decentralized, and it's an exciting space to be a part of.

Printed in Great Britain
by Amazon